Advance Praise for Christos Kartalis' *Performance Cockpit*

The first roo days are the most critical for a new general manager. Day one of any roo-Day Plan should include reading Christos' The Performance Cockpit, *an insightful, thought-provoking road map for success.*
- Dudley Schleier, Vice President, Pfizer Inc, Area President Japan/Asia

The Performance Cockpit *is an excellent, easy-to-read guide to excellence in management. It is profound that everything in the book has been implemented, tested and proven to work. Christos presents the key approaches of practicing general managers, offering succinct and straightforward advice.*
- Basil N. Tsaras, President and Managing Director, Prothesis Business Consultants, S.A.

As an American working for a Danish company in Turkey and now Australasia, I wish I had Christos' book years ago! It is a must-read, full of practical, implementable skills and tips for top managers in today's fast-paced global business environment.
- David Albachten, Managing Director, Novo Nordisk

Very few books provide readers with such insight and real-life experience. This book is a good road map to help understand what a "general manager" needs to do in order to optimize his chances of success.
- Michel L. Pettigrew, Chief Operating Officer, Ferring Group

This book is a comprehensive, useful guide that provides practical ideas and tools to sustain leadership success.
 – Dimitris Bourantas, Professor and Director of Executive BMS, Athens University of Economics and Business

Without execution, visions and strategies are worthless, an important lesson learnt from Christos Kartalis in The Performance Cockpit.
 – Bengt Westergren, Senior Vice President, AIG Companies, Corporate & Government Affairs

Practical checklist for every general manager in facing their new role during the first 100 days. Realistic and essential companion book for new general managers.
 – Liew, Yew Looi, Vice President, DKSH

From personal experience, Christos demonstrates how you can take complex strategic and operational challenges and distill them into tangible points of execution that ultimately drive success. There is no substitute for a track record.
 – Steve Walter, Vice President, IMS Health Consulting and Services, Asia Pacific

This book delivers real-life experience in a pragmatic approach, not an academic one. I know. I've competed with Christos and I can tell you, what he says in his book works!
 – Vangelis Georgakopoulos, Regional Director MEA/ Consumer Healthcare, Wyeth, Greece

Success is closely linked to setting stretched but still realistic expectations and targets. People drive performance and targets drive people. This is one of the many concepts well demonstrated in this book.
 – Frederic Ragmark, Chief Executive Officer, Medicover Group, Belcro Medical, S.A.

The New General Manager's

Performance
Cockpit

*Piloting your company to achieve your objectives
and outperform your competitors consistently*

Christos Kartalis

The New General Manager's Performance Cockpit

ISBN 978-9963-9373-1-8

Published by AylaVita
www.aylavita.com

Dad, we come from a country with one language, living in a country with a different language, and I am going to a school where a third language is spoken. Why?"

This is what our son asked my wife and me when he came back from his first day in the British kindergarten in Bangkok, Thailand, shortly after we moved there from Greece.

Six years, three countries, and several languages later, our son, Dimitri, and daughter, Kleio, had given up most of their weekends and holidays while I wrote this book. My wife, Matilda, kept our family together as I focused on making a career for myself.

I dedicate this book to these three special people

Contents

Legend

Quote: a single statement from the author, unless otherwise noted, that highlights a main point of the text

Remember: an important concept that makes a main-principle of the book easier to remember

System: a key system that facilitates the implementation of a key process

Testimonial: a real-life example that demonstrates the effectiveness of a system discussed in the book

Foreword

It's a pleasure to write a foreword to this book written by my friend and colleague in the business world, Christos Kartalis.

Christos is someone working today operationally in the business world. While he dispenses in large part with idle theories, he does not throw them all overboard. He is aware of what the business schools argue. He includes that in the analysis, but thankfully he focuses on real-world experience with case studies from executives with whom Christos has worked or met from other companies.

This book is of value operationally to men and women making their livings in business today. It is for all general managers who are struggling to make it happen, identify and fix a problem, and then deliver. In a nutshell, this book transforms concepts into winning strategies, all leading towards great and sustainable results.

Christos Kartalis shares the right first step: Handling management and headquarters and getting them on board to assist operational executives implementing change and growing business. If you can't get management on board, then you're going nowhere.

There is always the danger of becoming cynical though. After all, senior management can often be pretty dumb and unimaginative. Most publicly quoted companies are under quarterly pressure to meet financial targets set by the market. The budget process is like a ratchet, similar to the medieval rack, that CFOs use to "stretch" executives with stretched budgets. One can often compare the word "stretch" here with the word "cripple." That's why the key to success in one's love life…and in one's business life…is managing expectations…invariably downwards. Assessing what management wants and how this can fit into a realistic and achievable business plan is therefore the essential starting point to strategy.

Once management is on your side, the next step to effective business is collecting the resources: human resources, investment, product, and services. I increasingly feel that the key defining criterion for business success in the next ten years will be getting your human resources—your people—right.

And to manage those people, you need leadership. Now this word "leadership" has had more baloney and nonsense written about it than any other, with the exception, perhaps, of the word "vision." That's why we need a "convincing management platform," getting the right sources together under good leadership which then implements strategy in an effective and sustainable formula—a systems-based one.

Christos' book emphasizes the concept of a "convincing management platform." He clearly demonstrates systems to bring together the critical elements of any organization—its people, strategies, and execution.

Dr. Danny Thorniley
Senior Vice President, Economist Intelligence Unit
Vienna, May 2007

Introduction

Maybe you are a first-time general manager or plan to be one soon.

Maybe you are moving from one general manager's job to another, across divisions of the same company, across companies, or across geographies.

Maybe you are a division manager, sales and marketing director, or franchise head.

Or you are an entrepreneur who has the concept right and needs help in managing your ideas through.

Or maybe you are a leader of teams, regardless of rank.

Being the general manager of a company is one of the most difficult jobs a person can face in a career. It is rewarding and very challenging

The New General Manager's Performance Cockpit gives solutions to the challenges. It takes the complexity out of the job and guides you through beating the challenges.

It provides you with the skills and tools necessary for a strong, long-lasting, successful career. It shows you how to become "best in class."

It shows you how to run a tight ship by focusing on what really counts for consistently achieving your financial and leadership targets.

The Performance Cockpit contains strategies and systems for convincing, motivating, and aligning individuals and teams behind your strategy. In this book you will discover how to:

- Become a systems master while remaining flexible, adaptable, and expandable as you apply these systems to various situations and cultures.

- Excel in the art of focus and identify and prioritize what really counts. In the process, you will learn how to focus your valuable time on the important issues.

- Stand out from the crowd and advance your career faster by consistently outperforming your objectives, competitors, and the rest of your organization because you understand and act on trends sooner.

In each chapter, you will discover concepts that link vision, strategy, and execution. You'll experience systems that provide a common corporate language and culture-building, discipline, and trust while they align company objectives and define performance measurements that can be tested and compared.

The chapters include true stories and testimonials of good and bad management. They conclude with lists of takeaways that summarize the best ideas and concepts presented.

Everything in *The Performance Cockpit* has been implemented, tested, and proven to work. All the systems have been developed through the proactive approaches of practicing general managers who are still active in those roles.

Christos Kartalis
Paris, France

PS: After you read *The Performance Cockpit,* you will want to check out the sequel, *The Leadership Cockpit,* the systems-based approach that will help you lead individuals and teams, maximizing your personal and your company's performance.

1

There are two types of vision. Most companies have a vision that is passive, generic, and not close to strategy and everyday company life. Some companies' vision is executionary.
These are the ones that are going places.

What You Assume about Your New Job May Be Just Myths

Perhaps you have just moved into a general manager's position. Perhaps you have just moved to a new company, a new business unit, or a new territory. Perhaps you do not know the right buttons to push for a successful assignment. Do you know the myths of the job and how to avoid them?

This chapter will discuss these myths and misconceptions. By the end of the chapter, you will;

- have the necessary knowledge and systems to save valuable time and adjust quickly to your new job.

- know how to spot and avoid the traps.

- understand that sound systems are necessary to maximize the effectiveness and success of the Leadership you bring to the job.

Author's Case
The Author, Healthcare Company
Athens, Greece

I was excited! It was my first day on the job as a general manager for a division of the Greek affiliate of a multinational company.

13

I went to "Metamorphosis," the area of Athens where my office would be based. A representative from Human Resources was taking me from the third floor, where the President of the local affiliate held court, to the ground floor, where my office was located. I noticed an abrupt degradation in the office environment, but I did not make much of it... until we entered my new office. It was a filthy room, next to the copy machine. It had an old, dusty desk with one chair. (There were not even chairs for visitors!)

The almost see-through wall separators and the small window made it look like a prison. One would literally have to use a ladder to look through this window. Two old-looking computers sat in one corner. My office looked like it had been used as a warehouse of some sort.

My excitement subsided, and now I had a "what have I done?" feeling.

A nice cleaning lady came in and dusted off my desk while I contacted the computer department to request a PC. They told me they had one, but it couldn't be connected to the company's main system. They promised to figure something out soon.

They also told me that according to the company procedure, I had to wait almost two months to get a laptop delivered and set up.

Never mind about the excitement wearing down. I started feeling mad. And it was only 10 am, only an hour and a half into my new job! An hour and a half at the offices of "Metamorphosis" and the process of metamorphosis for me had already begun!

I hope the above personal experience is not a familiar one to you, but it is a good example of how poorly many companies, even multinational ones, are prepared for new management employees.

As an introduction to a systems-based approach to general management, here are the main myths that are associated with the job of general manager.

Myth Number One: "A tailor-made manual is waiting for you just by your office door"

Wouldn't be nice to get a thick manual on "How to go from A to Z" on your first day? How about a two-week training as well? OK, that might be too much.

How about having a couple of months of overlap with your predecessor so he can give you a systematic orientation, show you the ropes, and tell you what to focus on and what to watch for? This is not likely, either.

When they get the job, most general managers find out quickly that it is a lonely job—they are out there on their own. The previous person has been promoted or let go or taken his next career step. Usually, bosses prefer to let you "swim in the deep" from the start. They are always too busy for time-consuming tutoring.

Often, the leadership change was required quickly, yet the need for action is critical from day one. This is all the more likely when you are promoted or when you have advanced from within, and the transition period may barely be enough for you to discuss it even with your family, let alone prepare adequately for what is coming.

Unfortunately, most companies do not have the procedures or systems to develop people for one of their most important jobs. Even the best companies fall far short of offering tailor-made programs for general managers.

In this chapter and throughout the book, you will learn the Whats, the Hows, and the Whos for getting a head start in your new job, new company, or new assignment. Hopefully, you will avoid losing time reinventing the wheel and you can focus immediately on your priorities.

Myth Number Two: "If you have leadership, you have what it takes"

Well, first, do you have "It"? Can your leadership alone help you achieve your maximum potential?

Can personal leadership be compromised by the environment in which it is exercised?

Without doubt, strong leadership is critical. It is the most important factor in our success or failure.

Leadership can maximize performance and output when it is applied in an environment that balances the leader, the people being led, and the systems available for carrying out the leadership.

When these three parameters are working and well-aligned, leadership can flourish and make the difference between being a good and a great general manager

Otherwise, you risk being secluded in a leadership tower where you have little effect on overall performance and success.

What type of leader are you?

- You belong among the people who consistently and profoundly exhibit the leadership traits needed for the new job. In this case, it is relatively easy to adjust and adapt your leadership style and behaviors to the new situation.

- You are an aspiring leader, having shown the people around you that you have the "right stuff," at least in potential, and people around you (including management) believe that you have a good chance in pulling it through. Be cautious and careful. Don't assume that merely by taking the position or by learning from previous leaders, you have already mastered this subject, and don't expect that people around you will simply follow your lead. If you do that, you may find yourself very soon in front of your team, but not necessarily leading it.

- You might have been chosen for the job because of your strong functional skills or because of your past performance, but not because you have demonstrated the ability to lead through behaviors and systems. A common example of failing general managers relates to finance directors who move up to such a job. If you belong in this group, it is important that you acknowledge it. Then deal with it immediately through training, mentorship programs, and systems.

Myth Number Three: "Our company has training and development programs that will teach you all you need to know to be ready for the job"

Reflect for a moment how many people you know who have gone through such a program and became good general managers as a result?

If you find it difficult to come up with names, you are not alone.

We all have gone through so many trainings that it seems as if we have covered all possible subjects. There is no question about the value such learning can give you. Always keep in mind, however, the disadvantages these trainings can cause in creating sustainable changes of behavior and performance.

- Training must be implemented immediately in the field. Otherwise, you limit the value of the training to what is available from classroom discussion only. For example, remember all the Excel® and PowerPoint® classes you have taken only to find yourself seeking help from your assistant or colleagues on the same seemingly simple things.

- The leadership courses and programs available may not be linked to a well-monitored, on-the-job training and development plan. It is only on the job that you actually "learn," and only when you apply it to your daily work can you measure your understanding and your ability to apply what you learned in the trainings.

  Too often, the results of such trainings are not followed up, not even by immediate supervisors, let alone by a system designed in place for that.

- Training on technical or functional aspects of the job is easier to learn. Training on "softer" areas, however, is harder to master, and mistakes can be difficult to reverse.

Consider the simple example of listening skills, which is a common area for improvement for results-oriented, tough-minded managers in top positions. They know it and recognize it as a weakness but still have difficulty acting on it.

Myth Number Four: "I worked with a great manager and have learned everything from him"

You are indeed lucky and privileged. However, have you been able to absorb like a sponge from this person? Do you believe you have seen everything you will be asked to deal with?

Doing is far different from watching someone else do it.

Working next to a great manager is obviously one of the best ways to learn. People who demonstrate great leadership make work look easy and joyful, and they simply make us better.

If you are really good in absorbing, you go even further. You take different things from different people, select the very best from each one, and adapt the behaviors to your own style and situation.

You can also learn from bad management examples. Some people practice behavior and systems that just don't work. Do not underestimate the power of such learning, as it can give you some very good insights and hints about what *not* to do.

If everything is so positive on learning from a great manager, then why do we mention the above situation as a "Myth"?

The important concern is how you will apply these lessons when the environment changes. You may well find yourself in a new place, alone, with no support from that "great manager" and surrounded by people who want you to fail and prove that they deserved the top job instead of you: your management, your superiors, your employees, maybe even your company. It can get tough.

Another constraint is that the number of good examples tends to decrease as we advance to positions of higher responsibility on the corporate ladder

Myth Number Five: "My company has such great systems in place that it will be a breeze"

You are in for a big surprise!

Most company systems are institutionalized and corporate-driven. They are intended to help headquarters manage from the top down.

Just consider the systems your own company uses to manage numbers (budgeting, reporting, profit-and-loss statements, etc.), to conduct business reviews, or to apply controls and compliance policies, for example.

We are not suggesting that those corporate systems of managing downwards don't have merit. They do, and you should apply them to managing your teams as well as to fulfilling the expectations of headquarters. To maximize your effectiveness and achieve your potential, however, you need to use systems that are tailor-made for the job of the general manager. These should be easily aligned with the corporate systems but personalized enough so that you can stand out in your performance compared to other general managers and to your competitors.

One example of a system (or lack of one) is the brutal way head-quarters can apply the beautiful concept of "Think Globally, Plan Regionally, Act Locally" to their objectives. Headquarters often tend to selectively "think globally" or "plan regionally" or "act locally" and to exclude the other parts of the equation. In many cases, though, there seems to be very little awareness of having fully integrated strategies that can be sustainable over the long term.

Hedan's Case
Hedan Jerome, Business Unit Head,
Telecommunications, Paris, France

Jerome has had good experience on the concept of "Think Globally, Plan Regionally, Act Locally" and cautions us on the risks. He says, "I still have vivid memories of my participation in a two-day, company-wide European sales meeting. It was a prime example of non-coordination.

"The European Sales Effectiveness Head was taking us from workshop to workshop in identifying best practices which could be commonly applied across Europe, only to find himself (and also the rest of us) lost in the variety of different practices from country to country.

"Although we were all supposed to be using the same methods of sales management, it seemed like we were thirty-five different companies in one room."

Takeaways

- Being a general manager is a lonely job. Realize it early and put strategies in place to beat the odds.

- Don't waste time reinventing the wheel. Learn from others who have done it, from both their mistakes and their successes.

- Identify your personal leadership traits, then stress the positive ones, so you can stand out from the pack and maximize your personal and organizational performance.

- There is a big difference between classroom training and on-the-job experience.

- Working for a great manager and being out on your own are two different things.

- Most company systems are institutionalized approaches that mainly help headquarters manage downwards.

As you have seen in this first chapter, the road to success is not paved with roses. You need special kinds of skills to succeed.

Some managers are born with such skills, some develop them. Both can succeed. Other managers have them, further develop them, and go even higher.

Where are you in this skill-set ladder? What do you have to do to maximize your performance? Look into Chapter Two.

2

Leaders can be born or made.
If you don't have "It" but can develop "It," you can become
good. But, if you also have "It," you can become great.

General Managers:
Where Do They Come From?

Are general managers born? Are they made by developing in the process? Or are general managers automatically assigned to the top job? Is there a winning stereotype? Do all general managers have the same chances to succeed?

Understand the type of manager you are. You will adapt quicker to situations, distinguish yourself from the pack, lead compellingly, and win over employees and management on your way to top performance.

Know the importance of socio-economic background and the role it plays in success and career advancement. Learn systems and mechanisms to manage cultures and personal backgrounds proactively while maximizing your performance and that of your team.

Realize that you were chosen for the general manager's job not because you were the best qualified in one specific area but because you were probably the second best in most other areas. That way, you will keep your feet solidly on earth and improve your second-best qualities while you are reaching for the stars.

Let's First Define "Born"

Can a general manager be "born" as such? That sounds quite bold as a statement, doesn't it?

"Born" obviously does not refer to the actual act of giving birth to a child who has "leader" written on his/her forehead.

"Born" refers to the environment in which this person grew up, the degree to which he was influenced by it, and his chances to lead, team up, or follow. Moreover, it has to do with the opportunities he or she had to observe behaviors that would be useful for future roles.

It is not by accident that many offspring of politicians become good leaders, regardless of their chosen career. It is because they grew up in an environment where they saw, smelled, and lived leadership day and night.

Some people have better chances of becoming leaders because they have had this additional element throughout their childhood. This should not be taken lightly.

Can Leaders Be "Made"?

Wouldn't it be nice to be able to go to a training and three months later to be a first class leader? Something like a leadership pill that could transform you into a leader in an instant?

Sorry, guys, but it is going to be a little more difficult than this.

"Made," in this context, refers to people who seemed to have developed leadership traits, people who gained these capabilities through school or early work years.

George's Case
George Panagakis, Healthcare
Athens, Greece

George Panagakis, newly hired general manager of the Greek affiliate of a European healthcare company, came from a solid but conservative background, with both his parents being teachers. Through the years, he has been able to combine the humbleness and respect that his background brings with a ferocious aggressiveness in thinking and acting. These elements make a powerful combination.

What does he do to earn the "made" distinction?
First, he takes his job seriously, down to the last detail, with an extreme degree of ownership. He also sees learning opportunities in all things he is involved in, positive or negative. He uses highly supported and documented reasoning when he challenges people, thanks in part to his engineering background.
Most importantly, he consciously elevates his performance in all leadership behaviors to a higher level each and every time.

He is still too humble and respectful at times, and this keeps him away from bigger opportunities, but if there is one thing certain, he will move higher, sooner than most of us!

Most current leaders belong in this category: managers who have the intelligence to assimilate learning and to own it. They see every challenge as a classroom and view themselves as leaders-in-training who grab every opportunity to improve.

Can Leaders Really Be "Assigned"?

"Assigned"? Can that really happen?
Can someone be assigned to the leadership role? No, not really.
People can be assigned to a managerial job, but leadership is too personal a characteristic to be assigned.

Still, a large number of general managers are "assigned." These are people who simply happen to be there and are the best option for the job at the given time.

These managers are those who were the most "convenient" or safest choices at the time of search. So far so good. It gets dangerous, however, when these people assume that they are automatically qualified to be leaders simply because they were given the job.

These are often people who had already been working in the specific business unit for some time—possibly even old-timers. Management is entrusting the general manager's job to one of them mainly because it focuses on achieving a smooth leadership transition.

If the objective of having a smooth transition is the primary reason for which a person is internally assigned to the general manager's position, then the choice is wrong and will not work for the long term.

We can all think of examples where "convenience" and short-term thinking from management elevated the wrong people to top positions.

Daniel's Case
Daniel Barnes, General Manager
Fast-Moving Consumer Goods, Munich, Germany

Daniel reminds us that every time we get to a new job, a different set of weaknesses develops. A smart general manager identifies them quickly and makes extra effort to turn them into strengths that improve the performance and the survival of the company.

Daniel says: "I still have vivid memories of such a change when I was working in a canned foods company in the Munich area. After the voluntary departure of the gifted division manager, Martin, the previous finance and administration director took over the top job. Martin was an intelligent guy with good knowledge of numbers and quite good people skills (unlike what we observe with the average finance guys). Although he was good in hitting the short-term, numbers-related targets, he was never able to step up to the new challenge of managing the long-term viability.

"The newly hired director kept his focus mainly on monthly and quarterly performance, and pretty soon the longer-term neglect caught up with him and he was replaced."

These "assigned" appointments are the most tricky ones. Only a small number of people actually end up having a successful career. Most fail as soon as management stops supporting them or the bad results start catching up with them.

If you belong in this category, the first thing you need to do is realize it. Then do some extra work on your deficiencies in leadership before they catch up with you.

Are General Managers Black or White, Christians, Muslims or Buddhists, Men or Women, Americans, Asians, or Europeans?

Is there a winning combination of socio-economic background and personal traits for the perfect general manager?

Two candidates compete for an open general manager's position in Canada or Italy. Candidate A is a fifty-year-old Filipino, Buddhist, self-made division manager. Candidate B is thirty-nine years old, white, Christian, American, and the son of an ex-CEO of a Fortune 500 division manager of the same company. Who is more likely to be hired?

This theoretical comparison highlights the fact that it is difficult and challenging when the time comes for the final choice to be made for the selection of a general manager.

The example also demonstrates that, although great progress is being made in terms of equality and fairness, there is still lots of room for improvement.

Substantial bias still remains in the selection process. But once a person gets the job, his effectiveness is above and beyond any combination of race, religion, geographical, or educational background. If you deliver, your background matters very little.

Demographics of people should not be part of your evaluation of people's ability to achieve. Not by a long shot. Demographics need to be taken into account so we can ensure success. By knowing the background of the people around you, by accepting and respecting differences, you improve performance by understanding how people think and operate.

Let's take age as an example area

In general, younger people are expected to (and do) take more risks. They often act boldly, go deeper into issues, and challenge the status quo. They are easier to approach, they go beyond hierarchy levels, and they work fast.

Older people, on the other hand, have more experience in sizing up situations, more ability to balance difficult situations effectively, and more credibility as leaders due to their proven track record. They avoid jumping to early conclusions and do not make mistakes as easily.

Another example is related to culture

Asian culture is more indirect and more polite than Western culture. Asians generally have more respect for seniority of any type and a predisposition to solve problems without abrupt moves.

Significant cultural differences can exist within business units of the same company. Most of the time, the leader of a division creates a culture that shares many of the characteristics, values, and behaviors that this leader personally brings to the organization.

Self-Realization: Why You?

You made it. You got the job. Now what? You are confident you will do well.

But the two previous general managers before you were just as confident. The were both smart people with good track records and, it seemed, very good systems in place. The last one got promoted; the one before him was let go and, at the time, no one knew why. Some people thought it was his politics, while others thought it was because he went awry with his manager, who happens to be your manager now. Thus, qualifications on paper are not reliable tools to tell whether you will succeed. But you remain confident...

So why you? There were several good people in the short list. You don't know all of them but the ones you know are very good: Peter, George, Catherine...So why you?

It cannot be because you are smarter; Peter seemed as smart as Peter Drucker in your marketing meetings, while he is as witty as Woody Allen.

It cannot be because you are devoted and hardworking, because George has been in this company for sixteen years, long enough to pay for his devotion and hard work with two alimonies.

Can it be that you deliver consistently above expectations? Now, that might be, although Catherine was equally successful in exceeding financial expectations.

Then why? Why you?

It is simply because you have the best combination of all characteristics. You best promise to deliver results in the near term and to motivate people to work towards an even better company in the future.

You possess the functional and leadership capabilities for taking on this larger responsibility within the company. "Possess" is a key word. You have demonstrated behaviors that show you feel comfortable with the functional and behavioral requirements of the job, and management has the confidence to take the risk on you.

Promotion within the same company is the most common avenue of career advancement. People moving from department to department assume increased levels of responsibility until they finally become ready to assume The Job. In traditionally structured companies, people move from marketing or sales into a mid-management role (head of marketing or sales, for example, or both) and are naturally groomed for the general manager's job.

At other times, people come from totally different industries, not having followed the "expected" hierarchy movement but receiving the opportunity to show what management believes they can "do" in the future.

Amal's Case
Amal Naj, Healthcare
Bangkok, Thailand

Sometimes you have an ideal blend of cultures, geographies, and professional backgrounds that creates an almost unbeatable combination.

I met Amal Naj when we were both working in Thailand as general managers for the local subsidiaries of multinational healthcare companies. Amal was born in India and raised and schooled in the United States. In the process, he built a successful fifteen-year career as a journalist for the *Wall Street Journal,* interviewing people like Jack Welch and Larry Bossidy.

He also interviewed one of the top people at Pfizer, who saw enough in this aggressive, articulate, and results-oriented man that he hired him in Corporate Affairs. Amal moved up to the general manager position in Asia, where his exceptional performance recently took him back to headquarters as Vice President for Investors Public Relations.

You certainly can recall examples of rare individuals and companies who take those seemingly big risks by giving opportunities to people beyond normal hierarchy and career paths. Sometimes it pays off handsomely.

Whoever chose you for the job did so knowing what the needs of the organization were and who would be able to do the job best. They had expectations already in their mind, and they chose you as the person to meet and exceed those expectations.

Is it always as straightforward?

No, not always. Often, a specific appointment might also be part of management's plan to accomplish different objectives. When an international president appointed a person of Greek origin to the general manager's position in Turkey, he was sending a signal to someone that he was willing to take risks in developing businesses and people, contrary to cultural, historic, or religious beliefs.

It is easy to imagine that for most people with less risk-taking attitude and belief in leadership development, the candidate's origin could be a disadvantage. The great leaders out there, however, are smart enough to understand when and with whom to go out on a limb.

Promoted from within Versus Outside Hire

Were you internally promoted? Were you promoted from within the same division or were you hired from outside?

Is it important? Very much so. The more distance you travel to your new job, the bigger the challenge to make the adjustment period successful.

If you were promoted from within, it is much easier to make the transition. You already know the culture of the company and the operating systems, and you know enough of the politics to help you avoid the big traps. Knowing the culture, it is also much easier to find sponsors, these important people within management who talk positively on your behalf.

If you were hired from the outside, you need to do more work to get the information that will help you through the initial period.

You need to be softer in the beginning, feeling the ground and creating the necessary alignments and coalitions that will help you first establish yourself in your position. Then you move on.

Takeaways

- A leader can be "born" or "made" or "assigned." If you are of the third kind, you need to do more work to catch up.

- Age, gender and culture are not make-or-break characteristics. But by understanding where you come from and adjusting accordingly to the environment and situation, you can increase performance.

- You were chosen for the job not because you are the best in one area, but because you are the second best in most others.

- If you were internally promoted, don't take success for granted. If you were externally hired, work harder to catch up.

You have seen both that the background of a general manager is important to his success but not a condition *per se* and that everybody can make it. The next chapter dives into one of the cornerstones of general management—identifying management expectations.

3

The secret to success in one's love and business life is the same. Managing expectations, invariably downwards.
– Danny Thorniley

Go Where Your Boss Expects You to Go

Have you ever been in a situation where you were going one way and your boss wanted you to go a different way? Have you ever put priorities in a different order than management, causing you stress and additional work to get back on track?

Learning management's expectations of you is one of the first things you should do. Having objectives that are well defined, aligned with the rest of the company, and agreed-to by your boss keeps you focused. It helps you manage resources toward higher performance and achievement.

Clearly spelled-out and established objectives facilitate the process of planning for achieving them, leaving very little to misinterpretation.

When you get a new job or when your boss or the management above you changes, identify their expectations and get their agreement about your plans.

To fully understand expectations, find out clearly and concretely **what** your management wants from you, both for the short and long term.

Then check the **when**—how quickly they want you to deliver the "whats."

Finally, check **how** management wants you to deliver them.

You obviously had some idea about the main expectations before you even got the job. You probably discussed them during the interview process with the people hiring you and/or others with whom you consulted before you got the job. It was these expectations that the hiring people measured your competencies against when they finally decided to hire you.

Now that you've got the job, however, these expectations move from being part of the hiring process to becoming *the objectives!*

A discussion with your new boss is one of the first steps you should take in your new job. Ask him directly about what he/she expects you to accomplish. Ask him about the "what," the "when," and the "how."

Kanzaki-san's Case
Kanzaki Tohko, General Manager,
Logistics/Distribution, Tokyo, Japan

Kanzaki-san is a firm believer in getting the expectations from the boss. He emphasizes that the earlier you do it, the better.

He remembers: "Such a kick-off meeting has helped me prioritize on the right things from the start and save time and energy.

"I had just moved to Japan as GM of one of the largest logistics and distribution companies, coming from a similar position in a smaller market in Asia.

"My boss, President of Intercontinental, and I wanted to get together and talk about expectations during the one-day visit he made in announcing my appointment to the company locally, but due to tight schedules with groups of people for both, it kept on being postponed.

"From an after-dinner welcome drink on Thursday night to a breakfast meeting on Friday morning, to an early afternoon break to the ride to the airport for his flight back that evening... But I was not actually ready to let it go, so it finally took place in the small coffee shop at the airport just before his flight departed for London. We spoke about the 'Whats,' the 'Whens,' and the 'Hows.'

"Reflecting back, that twenty-minute chat was one of the most important meetings for this two-year assignment, as it clarified for me the objectives that my management was expecting for me to deliver, in which order and within what timeframe.

"Of course, it depends on what you can accomplish in twenty minutes with your boss but, I can tell you, twenty minutes with this specific person was equal to five hours of meetings, if you are smart enough to catch his every word and focus the discussion on getting as concrete answers as you can."

Regardless of where you have such a meeting or how much time you have available, make sure that you have one.

So, how do you run such a discussion?

Lead the discussion in a well-prepared manner. The more structured the discussion is, the better your chance of getting clear advice. Frame the discussion and target your questions around performance, systems, customers, and people.

What specific objectives are you expected to deliver? By when? In what order are you asked to deliver them?

What processes, systems, mechanisms, and teams should you be creating, improving, or dismantling to achieve the objectives?

What are the expectations for specific market segments? How do they want to see your relationship with customers develop?

First, Talk about *What* Management Expects from You

Does your boss believe that the company you have been chosen to lead is successful?

What makes it successful in his mind?

Does your boss expect you to make major changes? What specific investment decisions does he want you to tackle first?

Identify what he believes about the company while you are getting in the driver's seat. In other words, ask him to provide you with a brief SWOT analysis (SWOT: Strengths, Weaknesses, Opportunities, Threats). Ask him about his thoughts, ideas, and hints on how to tackle the main areas.

What type and size of numerical targets is he expecting from you?
Don't go for the exact numbers, but do try to get ballpark figures. For example, get an idea about the range of growth he expects.

Does he expect the company to be more or less customer-focused?
Identify what he believes about people and leadership and the extent to which the numerical part of your performance is more important than the "softer" parts (such as people and leadership).

Depending on his feedback, focus your attention and rank your priorities accordingly. For example, we all like to have leadership as the number-one priority, but if hitting your yearly profit target is the essential performance criterion for your boss, then you need to make that your priority. Otherwise, you create a conflict between your boss's priorities and yours: in this case, the numbers.

Second, Talk about *When* Achievements Are Expected from You

You know management's expectations as well as your objectives. Fine.

Now the next set of questions comes into play: do you have to accomplish the objectives over the short or the long term?

Furthermore, do you and your boss have the same understanding of what the "short" and "long" terms are?

Agreement on definitions (for example, "short term is a 4–6 month period") helps you prepare your action plan for achieving each objective by the deadline. A time-aligned plan always increases the chances for success. You also avoid these bothersome "reminder" phone calls and emails when you are behind your deadlines.

Once you have gotten feedback about *what* is expected from you, you need to map out the timeline. Break it down into the short term (3 to 6 months) and the long term (1 to 3 years).

Get enough information so you can map out and prioritize the expectations in detail, both in qualitative as well as quantitative terms.

Identify the quick fixes management expects so you can address them with the appropriate sense of urgency. These include the important issues that were left pending by the previous general manager and the changes that the company wants you to implement within a short time frame. Focus on those and start working on them right away.

Successfully accomplishing these short-term objectives will solidify you in your new position and give you the confidence and momentum to move into what is more important and critical for the organization: the long-term objectives.

Third, Talk with Your Boss about *How*

Is your boss willing and open to your implementing big changes?

Will he feel comfortable if you apply high levels of pressure to achieve the *whats* within the expected timelines?

Does your boss believe you have a magic wand or a remote control to fix everything in no time, easily, and without requiring anyone to shed a single tear?

Now that you know what the expectations are and when you need to deliver them, go into the more sensitive but equally critical area of *how* you are expected to achieve the objectives.

Get some guidelines about the level of change, the level of pressure, and the level of alignment your boss wants you to achieve.

In this discussion, identify the pressure you can apply in the organization and make sure management agrees and is comfortable with that.

Misunderstanding how you are expected to achieve the results can severely affect your performance and, in many cases, lead to your personal derailment.

It is an absolute fact! Many general managers charge into their new position like raging bulls only to realize some months later that they have been alone in this effort. In addition to losing support from within their organization, they lose management's confidence and head straight toward disaster.

You can see how easily beliefs and behavioral traits considered positive in the past can quickly turn into nightmares in the present... how readily your quick decision-making can turn into overly individualistic behavior... how quickly your aggressive style, something everyone once admired, can turn into what seems like authoritarianism... how your passion for hard work and getting the maximum of your subordinates can inexplicably lead to complaints of dictatorship.

*How can you get the right **hows** from your boss?*

Ask the right questions and make it easy for him. Give him options to choose from when he answers. Show your willingness to change your approach according to his priorities.

Management's View of Your Staff

Does your boss believe you have a good team?

Which people does he believe you should count on and, even more importantly, which ones does he believe are dead wood that should be removed?

Get some idea of how your direct reports in the future will be viewed by management. Find out who in your team are favored by management, who are considered indispensable, and who they have questions about.

Find out how they conceive of leadership in the organization you are asked to manage.

Then adjust your strategy and your execution to incorporate the thoughts and opinions you have just discovered. Give the toughest and most critical assignments to the people who are favored by your management as long as they perform at expected levels.

Do you always have to agree with your management about who deserves favor? Absolutely not. Be ready to challenge and to defend your decisions, but be smart when you do it.

Challenge management's opinion about people only when you know your people and when you have enough documentation of their abilities. Choose your fights with your boss very carefully if you don't want to risk losing your own credibility.

Knowing what management believes about your people will also clarify the extent to which you have the support of your team and the extent to which you should watch your back whenever you increase the pressure.

Takeaways

- Identify management's expectations. Do this right after you get the job.

- Get management to spell out expectations as clearly, qualitatively, and quantitatively as possible. In writing!

- Get your boss to tell you his view about your direct reports before you delegate important projects to them.

Knowing your boss's expectations is very important as you prepare your plans to become a successful general manager. An underlying but often underappreciated part of any good plan is its beginning.

Do well in your first 100 days. Start by reading the next chapter.

4

"How are things?"

This is one of the most strategic questions a general manager can ask his people.

If you use it consistently and you really mean it, people will open up to you and you will get information far beyond the weather conditions.

Your First 100 Days: More Important Than Anything Else

Do you feel confused? Do you experience so much pressure that you feel lost at times? Does it look like everything is important and needs to be done by...yesterday?

Every beginning is tough. On the one hand, you face many unanswered questions and urgent, pending issues.

On the other hand, you have insufficient time and information to do a proper analysis of each.

At times, it seems and feels like a series of endless tests.

Plan well, put the right systems in place, and watch your effectiveness increase three-fold.

Why 100 days?

Within the first three months on the job shows how well a new person will do and how successful he will be for the duration of his assignment.

By doing well during the first 100 days, you will impress employees, customers, and your boss. You will gain credibility and time for the duration of your assignment.

Another reason why the first 100 days are important is that during this period you have management "immunity," a grace period to make mistakes, to feel confused, even to ask stupid questions. Use this time wisely.

Systemize Your Way to Success with "The 100-Day Plan"

As soon as you know management's expectations and your time frame for delivery, put your action plan together into an easy-to-follow structure or map: your 100-Day Plan.

Share this plan with your boss and get his agreement so that he understands your approach, your focus areas, and your timetable and recognizes that you will manage your expectations in a timely manner.

The 100-Day Plan will:

- keep you focused and aligned.

- send the right type of messages to the organization in a balanced manner.

- give a solid and positive picture to your company as well as to outsiders.

- help you manage your agenda rather than letting others "manage" you into their own agendas by taking advantage of your limited knowledge during this beginning stage.

How can you prepare a successful 100-day plan?

- Select the focus areas you need to emphasize (department, function, or leadership) and identify the key contacts, the business

CHRISTOS KARTALIS / 100-DAY PLAN

AREA	SUBJECT	RESPONSIBLE	Jan 1	Jan 8	Jan 15	Jan 22	Jan 29	Feb 5	Feb 12	Feb 19	Feb 26	March 5	March 12	March 19	March 26
CULTURE	* Orientation	HR		XXX	XXX	XXX	XXX	XXX							
	* Meet direct reports individually in dinners/lunches								XX	XX	XX				
	* Meet sales teams														
ENVIRONMENT	* Industry and trends	Dept Heads	XXX												
	* Regulations, channels, pricing														
	* Key opinion-leading centers/people														
DEPT REVIEWS	* Reviews (see below)	Dept Heads	XXX	XXX	XXX	XXX	XXX	XXX	XXX	XXX	XXX	XXX			
	- HR														
	- Finance														
	- Sales														
	- Mktg														
	- Government affairs														
PROCESSES	* Meetings, processes	Previous General Manager													
HR ISSUES	* Profiles, salaries, incentive systems, hiring practices, benchmarking,	Human Resource Director									XXX	XX	XX	XX	
	* Trainings, development courses														
	* Leadership-development plans														
CUSTOMERS	* Top 5 customers	Sales & Marketing Heads						X	X	X	X	X	XX	X	XX
	* Industry leaders														
	* Government key contacts														
INDUSTRY ASSOCIATIONS	* President and board members	Gov't Affairs Head				XXX		XX							
PREVIOUS GENERAL MANAGER	* Pendings transfer	Previous General Manager	XXX	XXX	XXX	XXX		XX	XX	XX	XX				
	* Mentorship	Your Mentor													
BOSS	* Expectations	Your Boss	XXX												

NOTES
- **Dept Reviews:** All presentation/discussion material to be provided one day in advance for pre-reading/preparation
- **Presentations to include:** Historical update, Department goals (year), Top 10 priorities (month), Top 5 issues (quarter/year), Top 5 opportunities (quarter/year), Competition (all depts), Work/Projects in progress, Budgets, Benchmarking data (internal, external), HR Section on People
- **HR Presentation:** Profiles, Salaries/benefits strategy, Incentive systems, Hiring practices, Training/dev't, Leadership dev't, Benchmarkings

Ranking: - X: medium importance, XX: high importance, XXX: must (single Xs can be postponed while double and triple Xs have precedence in case of time unavailability)

reviews, the external environment, as well as any other important elements.

•• Identify the person(s) who is (are) responsible for each of the focus areas.

• Prioritize each focus area according to importance.

  •- Your "have to do's." These are the things you must not postpone for any reason.

  - Your "important to do's." You can postpone up to 30 percent of them when more important or urgent matters come up.

  - Your "good to do's." These are things you can do with a small delay. You can cancel up to 30 percent of them if timing becomes an issue.

  - Your "good to do eventuallys." Those are things you can do within the first three months for which the sequence is not important.

• Plan all activities on a weekly basis. A weekly time planner is one of the small secrets of success in this mapping. Adjust your plan every week.

Sean's Case
Sean Allen, Regional General Manager
Fast-Moving Consumer Goods, Hong Kong

Sean remembers how he missed prioritizing customers highly enough during his 100-day plan and how dearly he paid for it.

He says: "I had been a new general manager in Hong Kong for five or six months, doing quite well in terms of performance but facing increasing competitive pressure in our detergent line.

"I was having a business dinner with the owner of the biggest distribution company, basically asking for support in reversing the negative business pattern. With respect being very highly embedded in the Asian culture, this mild-mannered, older gentleman mentioned to me that our biggest competitor also assigned a new general manager for Hong Kong and, he added very emphatically, this general manager went to meet him and 'pay his respects,' as he put it, during only his second day in the city. He told me how impressed he was and how gestures like that can strengthen relationships. . . . The message was clear and I got it.

"I did remember that my first visit to this critical opinion leader took place only after I had been three months in Hong Kong and only while the first worrying signs for our products had surfaced."

Learn How to Listen and Gain Time and Credibility

Do you jump to conclusions faster than you should? Do you sometimes feel pressured to reply or to take a position prematurely, leading you to less effective communication?

You can improve your ability to provide well-rounded answers by listening attentively. Listening gives you the opportunity to develop a deeper understanding and to give better-articulated replies.

This is why, while you keep busy, you must have your listening antennas fully extended so you can continuously absorb the input you receive, especially during the first two or three months.

How you listen is critical. Listen carefully, avoiding making commitments about people or issues until you are sure about them. Avoid making commitments when you are not sure about the motives of the people who are talking to you.

Many people will come to you to help you out during your settling-in period. Distinguish among them wisely, and be wary of those who might have their own hidden agendas for approaching you. If you are like the rest of us and you need some time to reflect on messages and motives, listen to all but don't feel obliged to commit immediately.

Walk the Floor Effectively

How do you know what your people feel about your strategies? Are formal reports and business reviews enough? How do you touch hearts and feelings?

Learn to "walk the floor" effectively through a systems-based approach and increase your capacity to influence your people's performance as well your own.

Jonathan's Case
Jonathan Lohre, General Manager
Telecommunications, Boston, USA

Jonathan will tell you that failing to listen can cost you dearly.

He remembers: "I lost a good person by not reading the signals early enough.

"I had the habit of 'walking the floor' twice per week, chatting with the colleagues. The marketing assistants were always insightful in giving me good updates, but I missed catching the comments of one of them. She was receiving lots of complaints about our invoicing system from the southeast regional manager, a very capable and strong leader with consistently good performance.

"I thought it was just a case where a very busy person complains about the workload. I did not go deep enough to remember that she mentioned it to me at least two times during my past one-minute discussions with her.

"Two months later, this regional sales manager left the company out of frustration, as delays in deliveries to her area due to poor invoicing were affecting her performance and, obviously, patience.

"I did not listen well and early enough, and we lost a good employee to a competitor. It took us three months to fill the position and almost double that time to get performance back on track in her region."

Here are some simple tips that help you towards touching more hearts and minds

- Plan it well. Do not leave it to "whenever you have some free time to walk around." Put in your calendar the objective of visiting specific areas or departments two times per week. That way, you will establish the interaction and the frequency necessary to make the impact you desire.

- Clarify your "walking the floor" objectives. Don't "walk the floor" without specific objectives in mind. Think of the specific people you want to see, the things you want to discuss with them, and the kind of message you want to give them. With some people, you might follow up on a project they are working on. Your interest will recognize their efforts and show that you are a hands-on manager. They might even tell you how well they think they are doing so you can give them a pat on the back.

- Say hello to everybody you see on your way. Talk to everyone as you walk by. Say hello and talk about the weather, their children's school, or any other subject. The important thing is to talk to them. Be approachable and people will appreciate it.

- "What's new?" Even if you don't have time to prepare for meeting everyone when you are "walking the floor," you can always ask simple questions:

  - How is everything?
  - What's new?

- Stand across from the people you talk to, look them in the eyes, and ask questions as though you really want to know the answer. A simple question like "what's new" can take a whole new meaning for the person you are talking to. Even if they reply with a "things are quite busy but we are doing okay" type of answer, inquire more. Ask them "what are you working on?" and show genuine interest in their feedback. The results will be fantastic.

The more systematic your approach to "walking the floor," the more effective your impact will be

Visit each department to chat at least twice per week. Each time you visit, have in your mind some things you would like to talk to specific people about. These could be related to work (project follow-ups, etc.), but they are more effective if you talk about personal things. Ask your assistant to keep you informed about personal events like births, birthdays, and deaths in families, and talk with the people one-to-one about them. These special discussions can have a long-lasting effect if done consistently.

- Have one-to-one lunches with each of the people who report to you directly. Get to know them in a friendly environment and open fashion. Give them face-to-face interactions with the new head. Listen to them. If you let them speak more than 60 percent of the time, you will have done pretty well.

- Have informal lunch meetings with all your colleagues of small departments or functions. I always have fruitful discussions during lunches that I hold twice a year for the secretaries of the company. Chatting about work and their ideas about improving the company, for example, can go a long way with your image and your effectiveness.

- Seek out specific people and talk to them periodically. Ask those who report directly to you to tell you who should be included in this group. It could be the high-potential employees whom you need to keep motivated or recognized. It could be the two or three guys leading important projects, so show your confidence and pump them up. It could be some people on derailment.

- Be enthusiastic. Smile and show strength and calmness to everyone who sees you or talks to you in these formal gatherings—or even in the coffee room or by the water cooler. Always keep a nice, short, and positive summary of the main events in your mind so you can ask the specific people who are responsible for those and get them interested.

Effective Job Hand-Over

Depending on the complexity of the job, the hand-over from the previous general manager should be done in a well-organized and timely implemented manner.

Ideally, the outgoing general manager will be available to act as a "consultant" instead of remaining actively involved in operational matters, which could create issues on leadership, disorient the organization, and undermine the efficiency of the new general manager in this first, critical period.

Christopher's Case
Christopher Foster, General Manager
Telecommunications, U.S.A

Christopher reminds us that a bad hand-over can be more damaging than when there is no handover at all.

"In my company, it was quite normal that the hand-over period would be minimal to zero. Since the outgoing manager was not to move to his new posting in the headquarters for a couple of months, it was decided that he would stay in Boston with me to assist in my transition.

"At first I found it to be a really good idea, especially since that was my first general manager's posting. I soon realized, however, the negatives would outweigh the positives by far.

The outgoing general manager continued to be involved in all matters, interacting directly with my people to the extent that most of them would overpass me and continue to go directly to him for advice. When I started to assume personal ownership of situations, plans, and people, he would get upset and would show it to all, locally as well as to the regional management.

That month was one of the most difficult months in my career, not so much from the job-content point of view but due to the fact that I was under continuous surveillance and criticism.

"In all honesty, I would have preferred that the company stayed firm in its initial method of minimizing the hand-over time to zero."

Make All Decisions on Pending Issues

Do you have piles of issues waiting for you to handle? Does almost everything seem to be urgent? Do you feel like the people are looking at you with that look that demands solutions...quickly?

It is normal that during your first days on the new job, you will have to deal with lots of pending issues, including problems that have remained unsolved or situations left unclear from the previous administration.

This could be partly due to logical and normal events. The absence of decision-making authority at higher levels is more common during transition-of-power periods.

It could also be related to bottlenecks created in processes and departments. Without authority figures, imbalances among departments can result when authority or power are redistributed among the department heads during transition periods. Unfortunately, such vacuums and bottlenecks lead to confusion and decreases in morale and impact heavily on productivity.

While you go through the orientation period, it is crucial that you show right from the start that you mean business.

Resolve all pending cases and let everyone know that you intend to achieve results with speed and decisiveness.

At the same time, send a message to your upper management that the transition is running smoothly.

Start by finalizing all the decisions that are pending from the previous administration.

Ask your department heads to provide you with a prioritized list of pending issues and act on them promptly. That way, you will free up bottlenecks while you assist the department in keeping up a good pace of performance.

You will also give the strong and positive message to your organization that you are ready to make the decisions and take the risks with the speed you would like to see the organization achieve.

Antonio's Case
Antonio Morales, General Manager
Investment Banking, Spain

Antonio notes that the pile of pending matters is created not only by the previous general manager's inability but also by the outgoing manager' risk-averse behavior during the last part of his assignment. In both cases, the price to pay is high.

"I had taken over from a general manager, a slow-paced, smart, but politically inclined fellow, who had literally not made a decision for the past three months. He was too preoccupied with his own promotion and was not keen to take any risks during the last months on the job.

"Pending issues ranged from important human-resources issues, to replacement of PCs for the accounting department, to the signing of key contracts.

"In that case, we missed out on the opportunity to hire some very good people; they had flown away to the competition due to the delay from our part in replacing the three to four people in critical positions who had been identified for replacement.

"Everything was conveniently left in the pendings tray for the new general manager. We paid for it."

When you encounter situations like that, do not worry. It could be a blessing in disguise, an opportunity for you to show early on what you are made of and how you are going to manage. Take the opportunity to send early signals and to establish yourself quickly as a strong and decisive new leader.

How to handle bottlenecks effectively

- Identify and list all pending matters and bottlenecks through brief brainstorming sessions and one-to-one meetings with your direct subordinates and others.

- Prioritize them according to importance in terms of impact on the business.

- Appoint small project teams, each consisting of two to four people, to analyze and provide recommended options. Give them a short deadline. If you need to, go below the level of your direct subordinates to identify the problem or to find the right people for the team solving the issue.

- Fully support the team and closely monitor execution as you implement the recommendations.

- Rcognize and reward people for their participation, especially if the results are successful.

Although in most cases the transfer from the previous general manager is incomplete, the opposite is also possible. A general manager who has done a fantastic job leaves little to be improved. That, in a strange way, could also be an issue, as you will find it rather difficult to identify areas to improve and show your capabilities, at least in the beginning of your assignment.

Talk with the "Past"

Talk with some of the key people who have left the organization. Approach people who have either left on their own for a new company or talk with the ones who were let go by the previous management.

Why is it important to talk with these people? First, they have no reason to hide anything anymore, but they will feel valued that you are talking to them.

Most people will be glad to meet with you. They will appreciate your interest in taking their views into account. They may well be eager either to show that the company was wrong to let them go or to share ideas they want to help the company with.

Be extra careful to take disparaging comments with a grain of salt if you feel that the people are biased or seeking revenge on their previous management or colleagues.

This technique is particularly useful when you step in after a crises or a troublesome event (e.g., a big management shake up).

Rocket science is not required to get the right feedback. Classical leading questions could include:

- Why did you leave?

- Would you come back again?

- Would you recommend our company to your best friend?

- What two or three things did/do we, as company, really do well?

- What things can we do better?

It is equally important to talk to customers
Identify customers who will give you direct and honest feedback. Meet with them in informal, relaxed gatherings, such as dinners

and lunches. If you choose the right people, then you will get the right answers back. Ask them:

- What are the three best companies in the industry, excluding my company?

- Where would you put my company in terms of ranking?

- What are two things you like about our company?

- What are four things you would recommend that we improve?

- What is our company image?

- What do you think about our people and systems?

- Are we fast or slow, ethical or unethical, conservative or contemporary, leaders or followers?

Take Aways

- During the first 100 days, you might feel confused, lost at times, overloaded, overworked, lonely. Knowing that this is expected is half of the answer. The other half is having a tight "100-Day Plan" in place.

- How well you do in the first 100 days will show you and others how well you will do for the rest of your assignment. It will feel like a series of endless little tests. Plan appropriately and pass them all.

- For the first 100 days, use 75 percent of your time to prepare and listen and 25 percent to execute. Open your mouth only when you have something important to say. You will have ample time to talk later.

- During the first 100 days you have management "immunity," a grace period to make mistakes, to feel confused, and to ask stupid questions. Use this time wisely.

Now that you know the importance of a good early start in each assignment, let's dive into it more. In Chapter Five you will see how you can make a big impact during this first period through leadership and systems.

5

Challenge the obvious.
Here, most of the opportunities lay.

Focus Internally Rather Than Externally First

Do you know whom in your new team to trust with high-priority projects? Do people resist your ideas just for the sake of resisting, causing delays in the execution of your plans? Do you feel confused and energy-drained at times by everything you have to do within a limited amount of time?

In this chapter you will see the importance of focusing internally at first, and you will then learn how to do it.

When you focus internally during this first period of your assignment, you will show the type of a leader you are and you will gain hearts and minds quickly.

Increase efficiency by identifying early who are on board with your plans. When you empower them, you will increase the impact of your messages across organizational layers.

When you work harder, longer, and more intensely in the beginning of your assignment, you will gain time, followers, and productivity.

Rank Your People According to Their Ability to Align to Your Strategy and Leadership Style

As a newcomer, you cannot know the people around you.

What makes them stop and go? What makes them tick? What motivates them?

These are all good questions. *Where do you start?*
Begin by categorizing your people according to their willingness to align with your strategies and your management style.

Which people are we talking about?
People at various levels in the organization with high authority and/or influence. People about whom you personally have formed an opinion or about whom you have heard from colleagues whose opinion you trust.

List these individuals, then rank them according to their willingness to align with you and the time it will take them to do it. The more they are willing and the shorter the period, the better.

Place your priorities on the shoulders of those who are most willing to work with you.

As for the rest, the ones who will resist, neutralize their influence and, if needed, remove them from the organization.

Following are the kinds of people you will encounter as well the methods you can use to manage them:

"Early Adopters": These are people who crave something new They are open to new ideas and see newcomers as a chance to break the monotony.

They are usually young people, well educated, still at lower management levels but very ambitious, confident about their abilities, and eager to prove themselves to anyone who comes to lead.

These are the so-called "drivers." They are found in most companies in small numbers, about five to fifteen percent of the work force.

"Mid-Range Adopters without effort": They are easy to gain on your side. They are mostly positive thinkers who welcome something new once a period of time goes by and they are reassured that you are not insane, risky, or unpleasant to be around.

Pay them some personal attention; they will quickly come along. They have typically been with the company for two to four years,

ADOPTION MAPPING OF KEY PEOPLE, ACROSS 90 DAYS

Willingness to Adopt: High — Medium — Low

Time Period: Day 90 — Day 45 — Day 1

Categories (with Day 1 and Day 90 points):
- Early Adopters
- Mid-Range Adopters without effort
- Mid-Range Adopters with effort
- Late Adopters
- The Impossibles

Guidelines
- Have one line to show how the situation is on day 1
- Have one line to show your realistic expectation of where they should be after the 90 days.
- According to level of improvement, you decided to either:
  a) count on them by giving them more responsibility
  b) neutralize them and focus working with the more willing group
  c) proceed towards more drastic action such as reassigning to a new role or consider dismissal

long enough to reach mid-management levels. They like what they are doing, they are established in their positions, but they still have ambition to advance.

They are open to try new things provided you are successful during the initial "probationary" period they give you. They represent about twenty percent of your people.

"Mid-Range Adopters with effort": If these people are part of management, they will eventually align with you, but it will take some work from you for this to take place. Spend some time with each of them, show them signs that you are open and positive, and find out their personal reasons for joining with you.

If these people are in administrative, clerical, or low-management positions—those who do the job for the bread and butter and care little about who is in charge as long as they get their paycheck on time—things are different. These people may have nothing to gain or lose from management change. They may have little interest to jump in and little reluctance to follow. The term most commonly used in describing those people is "residents."

About thirty percent of your people will fit in this category.

"Late Adopters": This is the tough crowd. They are always critical of change and skeptical of newcomers, and they often think they already know it all. Having been in their positions longer than the average employee and having seen new bosses as threats to the small castles they have built, they may give you a hard time. Be patient with them, show them some respect, and hit the right buttons to get them on your side. Eventually they will come around, but do not expect them to be the movers and shakers. Ten to twenty percent of your people belong in this group.

"The Impossibles": They will never come along, either because they were the favorites of the previous administration, because they see you as a threat to the small worlds they have created for themselves, or simply because they don't like the way you talk, or walk, or…

If they are part of management, identify them and take them out, quickly and smoothly.

If they are part of administration and the clerical staff, take out the ones who can negatively influence other employees, and do not worry too much about the rest.

Remember, you will never be able to win them all, not even for an hour, so focus on wining the ones that count.

Focus Internally First

Is it difficult to balance your focus among burning issues? Do you have too many requests from headquarters, complaints from customers, or aggressive actions by competitors?

A normal workday is eight to twelve hours. When you are new on the job, it would be impossible to capture everything, even if the working hours expanded to twenty hours per day. So, what do you do?

The first thing is to set up your priorities according to the "100-day plan" as described in an earlier chapter. That way, you will have a good understanding of the situations, problems, and opportunities at hand, and you'll get a pretty good feel for the people around you.

In order to maximize your impact, however, you need to focus internally first.

Cultivate a good handle of the situation inside your company before you start investing considerable time on the outside.

Here are some important techniques and special tools to help you organize and systemize your approach:

Spread around the concept of "0-base"
Set everything back to a theoretic beginning base and start with the question: "If I were to start this from zero, how would I go about it? What would I do differently?"

This can profoundly affect the way your people think and act. It can be very useful when you challenge proposals or rationales.

Will people resist when you start spreading the concept of "0-base"?
Of course they will. People will feel criticized and try to defend their "status quo." This is to be expected. Most people feel obligated to defend plans or structures that they have created or been working with for some time.

Select one or two departments as a test. These departments should be chosen because of the openness of the head of the department and/or key managers to try this without feeling threatened.

Take all processes, investment rationales, and strategies, and ask the simple question: "If you were to start this from scratch, what would you do differently?"

Daeun's Case
Daeun Lee, General Manager
Logistics/Distribution, Seoul, Korea

Daeun warns that the rollout of the "0-base" concept will result in surprised, red faces and blank stares on the people across from you.

"I vividly remember examples of people being astonished about how this approach can change their thinking.

"I was a couple of months into my new job when the head of collections came to my office to recommend an increase in the bonus plan for the collectors.

"You could see his face getting red when I asked him to justify why we actually give bonuses to collectors, since they cannot affect timing or the amount of receivables but were merely receiving the checks from customers and delivering them to our bank for deposit.

"He seemed to be fainting away when I asked him to do an analysis of replacing the collectors with an outsourced service, such as factoring.

"'0-base' can be used for important issues related to infrastructure and human resources, to resource allocation, as well as to smaller-impact issues like purchasing policies and hotels.

"Our small purchasing department saved about $200,000 simply by announcing a '0-base' to our suppliers and requesting specs from other suppliers. Effort? Nothing more than twenty to thirty phone calls and lots of '0-base'!"

Benchmark what really counts

Do you have the right plans in place to ensure the highest productivity?

Do those plans bring the optimum level of return on investment? How do you know?

People try to create the "ideal" company in their mind, especially when it is related to benefits.

When people are talking about a new-car policy, they will bring as an example the company that allows BMWs for sales representatives or the one that has extravagant incentive plans, such as paid trips to the other end of the world and back. The same goes for salaries, bonuses, work hours, and everything else.

Employees would still be complaining even if, compared to the rest of the industry, they had the highest salaries and bonuses, a Jaguar, three months of vacation per year, and guaranteed promotions every two years. No matter what the benefits are, people would eventually find reasons to complain! Guaranteed!

Credible benchmarking data can assist you in finding the optimum level of investment.

Ideally, anything that you set as an objective or a benchmark must be quantifiable, measurable, and comparable. Otherwise, it should not be an objective.

The data to be used in such benchmarking are selected with regular frequency. For example, compensation surveys and employee-benefits comparisons can help you develop a well-founded human-resource strategy and support your decisions during your discussions and conflicts with employees.

Such data can be collected from industry surveys or associations, studies that your company initiates, and internal studies from company headquarters. To make your work easier, develop a list of benchmarking areas.

Let's take the department of human resources. The following is a list of areas an HR department needs to benchmark:

- Compensation plans
- Car policy
- Hotel lists
- Mobile policy
- Training and development plans
- Employee turnover statistics
- Employee diversity (gender, color, nationality)
- Promotion and grading systems
- Retention plans
- Career and succession plans

Do a systems check

Such a check could vary from a quick, informal audit of compliance all the way up to an examination of employee motivations.

Look into the status and strength of the systems that affect output in each major area. For example:

Performance factors: Check into areas of objective setting, target allocation across products and departments, achievement monitoring, participation across different departments in goal achievement, amount and status of receivables, and sales trends of your key customers versus your main competitors.

A simple, one-page "aging analysis of your receivables" will tell you more than meeting with each collector for a day!

People: Compare key elements of culture, management philosophy, and styles (autocratic versus participative). For example, teamwork, alignment with objectives, departmental staff turnover, etc.

Check the motivation by looking into the target achievement versus targets per department. In most cases, a motivated team is one that achieves targets and does so consistently.

Compliance history: Who did what, how did the company handle compliance cases in the past (with softness or toughness, for example), how frequent were the incidents of non-compliance, etc.

Processes/systems: Look at forecasting, inventories, and collections. It is equally important to monitor the reports to your local management team and to upper management. Check the quality of reports such as formal budget documents, follow-up processes, monthly reports, participation reports, and other budgetary documents.

Customers: Look at the formal/informal systems used to keep in touch, research studies, and study budgets. Pay special attention to product returns and service or product complaints. Check variations in things like seasonality factors and variances per product or service line.

Consumer complaints can give a quick but very good overall idea of how well your company is really operating.

Clear the bottlenecks

Bottlenecks are everything that slows the organization down. These are usually areas where responsibility is not well defined and/or the solution to an issue does not fall into an existing process. Bottlenecks can compromise the ability of your organization to perform and lead to both misalignment and loss of momentum.

If you can clear the bottlenecks, you will get back much more than you asked for. You will give a clear signal to your people that you mean business, provide speed to the organization, and even save some money.

But clearing bottlenecks has to be done with diplomacy. You don't want it to be seen as a control measure or check-up procedure.

Sometimes the bottlenecks are right there in front of you, crying out for someone to step in. Most of the time, however, they are embedded so deeply in the status quo and routines that you need to do some digging to get them out.

Make it be and look like double time

Consider this scenario. Immediately after your appointment is announced, you take the first plane up to a height of 20,000 feet where you can exercise what the theorists of this world call the secret to success: "Taking a 20,000-foot view of things." You focus on strategizing and leave execution to others. You delegate authority to such a degree that your personal involvement in execution is minimal.

What do you think will happen?

Chances are you are not going to be there for long. The same plane that took you up to 20,000 feet will take you down...fast!

How can you avoid the fall?

First, consider the new job as an opportunity, a great chance to *set the tempo* according to which you would like to see things run. It is as if you were in the first five minutes of an important basketball game and setting an example of how you, the playmaker, will start the game, how fast or slow you will run the team, how aggressively or softly you will play, how risky or careful you will be. The rest of your team will react accordingly. Five minutes into the game, we seem to know who is going to win, don't we? Setting the tempo is critical.

Show to all the speed at which you like your division/company to run.

- Be the *first to arrive and last to leave* the office. Make an early start in the morning and stay after normal working hours. Give the signal that you mean business.

- *Hard work* is not bad time-management when you turn it into a competitive advantage. No one should be working beyond nine to five for the company alone. You do it for your career, for yourself.

- When you *work late at night or even into the weekends,* do it because you want to improve your performance, to stand out from the crowd and thereby to improve your career. If you see this extra work under this light, it becomes easier to accept. You can do it with more enthusiasm and achieve better results.

- *Arrive punctually* at meetings. Show respect to other participants and to the meeting organizer.

- *Be visible.* Participate in as many company events as possible, talk to people, give them the opportunity to talk to you and express their views, concerns, or ideas.

- *Be personable.* Answer all internal emails, not only the ones that are addressed to you but also the ones on which you are copied. This is an opportunity to bring people closer to you. Acknowledge receiving the email, appreciate the effort, offer suggestions, and always thank the person for their focus and follow-up.

- Once you know management's time expectations or deadlines for their various requests, plan to *break the time to achieve in half!* This includes achieving major milestones, replying to headquarter's requests, and to the personal effort you are putting into your new job.

Make your presence felt from the start

Make your presence felt from day one. Do the simple things that demonstrate change, decisiveness, and leadership. Do them from the very first day.

Identify what the *previous GM did not do or did less adequately.* Then do more than he did.

Some people have done this successfully every time they have gotten a new assignment. It has worked beautifully each and every time.

For example, if your predecessor did not participate in company sales meetings or events with customers, make it your priority not to miss a single company event. The difference will be obvious.

Other cases may be less obvious, such as cases of discrimination. Suppose women have not had equal opportunities in the business. It would be easy to make a noticeable difference from the beginning by giving a generous number of first recognitions or promotions to women.

Takeaways

- Gain time and efficiency in your new role by ranking your people according to their willingness to cooperate with your leadership style and plans.

- Identify and limit the influence of the people who don't align with you. Limit the resistance and ensure that willing employees get on board faster.

- Keep a major career competitive advantage by working hard. It's not bad time-management. In the first months on the job, working hard will help you gain time and efficiency.

- Do what your predecessor did not. Show your people early on that things have changed with your leadership.

In this chapter you saw that lots of smart and hard work is required in the first period of your assignment. The next chapter shows how you can make this work visible, understood, and appreciated by those around you. Make these first impressions your best impressions.

6

Good, systematic early starts guarantee the final win in almost all cases.

If in doubt, check the statistics of basketball games.

The team that wins the first quarter has a much higher probability to win the game.

Make the Best Impression Early: Listen to Others' Feedback

Can you recall situations where you created a bad impression? Would you like to be able to turn the clock back and change the perceptions people have of you? Do you know that you have a golden chance to substantially improve your image with your new assignment?

All impressions are important, but the first ones are the most crucial. They create the base for people when they meet you. Impressions lead to perceptions, and perceptions are the key component of your success or failure. Once you create perceptions, they are difficult to change. This is why it is important to manage those first impressions well and create long-lasting, positive perceptions.

In this chapter, you will discover the power of first impressions and discover methods and tools to present yourself in the most effective way. You will learn how to build fast rapport with those around you and to create quick connections—all in keeping with your business objectives.

Through effective use of systems, you can show to others your beliefs in fairness, compliance, and strategy.

Right from the beginning, you will demonstrate who you are and what it will be like when you are in the cockpit.

Importance of First Impressions

Admit it! Like most people, you have been in situations where you have subconsciously formed strong feelings of like or dislike about people the instant you met them.

Remember the last time this happened at a meeting or a social occasion. Remember the way they talked, their style (friendly or arrogant), their initial comments, their emotional distance from you, etc.

Regardless of the reason behind these first impressions, one thing is certain: your initial impression of someone will stay with you for some time. What is also certain is that it will require a large amount of effort to change that initial impression.

Consider what happens when you interview someone. Many people will admit that during interviews, they make up their mind about hiring or not hiring a person during the first five to ten minutes of the interview. They spend the rest of the interview fitting the candidate into the favorable or unfavorable box in which they placed the person during the initial few minutes.

It could be because of instinct, our ability to read people, our experience, or a combination of those that we judge and categorize people from the first glance.

The fact is that first impressions are critical. If we manage them correctly, they can become a major part of our strategy to win people to our side quickly.

Pay attention to presenting yourself in a positive way.

How well do you prepare for creating those first impressions and messages you give to others during your first days in your job?

What tools, systems, and ideas will help you excel in this direction?

The three systems below will help you make your first impressions more favorable than ever before:

"Teachable Point of View"
"Walking the Talk"
"New-Leader Assimilation"

"Teachable Point of View"

What are your core values and beliefs?

Would you like others to know about them before they form their first impressions about you?

The objective of this tool is to provide others with a snapshot, a picture, of you that features the deeply rooted beliefs and behaviors that have shaped you over the years.

Make a personal list of your values, beliefs, and behaviors. The simpler your list—one-liners or bulleted items, for example—the better. Don't make it a laundry list; try not to go over seven or eight items per section (see below).

The "Teachable Point of View" is comprised of three sections:

IDEAS: What are the concepts and ideas that you use on a daily basis, including your beliefs about people, customers, work style, and decision making.

VALUES: Are you a team player or do you believe in strong, single leadership? Are you formal or informal?

EMOTIONAL ENERGY: This is my favorite part. What makes you get up early with a smile as you face a hard day? How do you balance the needs of the organization and the important aspects of your life?

When and how to communicate your "teachable point of view"

Communicate it throughout your first three months on the job. Communicate it consistently and relentlessly in all directions. Include your main points selectively in formal speeches as well as in meetings and informal discussions with your target group.

Christos Kartalis' Teachable Point of View

Ideas

- Dominate categories where the Number-one position has been achieved.
- Grow products within the three leading products in each strategic category.
- Let the consumer lead.
- Be proactive on change, lead it, don't let it lead you.
- Prioritize objectives, strategies and tasks....and *focus*.
- Look for the 80/20 rule.
- Choosing to work next to excellent people brings up my level of productivity as well.
- Benchmark on each point and subject.
- THE GAME IS CALLED: MOST EFFICIENT ALLOCATION OF RESOURCES.

Values

- It is a team's work, results, and reward.
- Create an environment of confidence in the leader out of trust, not out of insecurity and fear.
- Think big. Continuously search for the dominating business idea.
- Be direct/honest/no politics.
- A strong culture is preferred to organizational charts and manuals.
- Informality fares better than tight control and increases accountability.
- Allow room to test, to try new things, even to make mistakes, always adhering to the targets.
- BE ENTHUSIASTIC, SMILE!

Emotional Energy

- "Let's do it now" attitude (Ready-FIRE-Aim versus Ready-Aim-Fire). Perfect information might never come and, if it comes, it will almost never be on time.
- Working hard and long is not necessarily bad time-management but personal competitive advantage.
- Lead by example.
- Empower people at all levels.
- The job, the result, and the reward are each person's baby.
- Provide maximum visibility for people working for me.
- Be a team player: either lead the team or work under a strong leader/decision-maker.
- Don't carry "dead wood." Don't let those who don't contribute stand in the way of productivity and growth. It is not fair to the company and other "fast movers."
- There is still lots of room to find a final path.
- CONSTANTLY CHALLENGE MYSELF AND OTHERS.

Communicate your teachable point of view to people at all levels in your division and company.

Do the same with customers and other key stakeholders, such as government officials, business associates, consultants, agencies, and banks.

Incorporate parts of the teachable point of view in all your discussions with employees and especially with your direct reports. Ask them how they feel about what you share and what their own teachable points would be. You'll find common points you can build relationships around. Communicate your points of view verbally during company meetings by including them at every opportunity.

The most effective way to communicate your point of view, however, is to set aside a two-hour meeting with your direct reports and the top personnel in your unit or company where you can have a good discussion of your teachable points.

Put the document up on the projector and give examples from your past to make each point better understood.

Ask the audience to tell you some of their own stories whenever someone identifies with a specific point.

You can also open the floor to questions and concerns, but do this carefully. It can derail the discussion towards negative areas, and this is not what you want to do.

Every general manager should develop his own teachable point of view.

Make a first draft, test it with the people around you to make sure you have included all the major points, and then put it to work, communicating to people around you whenever you have the opportunity.

"Walk the Talk"

Everybody will be watching you—your employees, your management, your customers.

They'll be paying attention to what you say and what you do. Most importantly, they will be monitoring the differences between what you say and what you do.

They will watch with interest how you react the first time when you need to make tough decisions. It is exactly those first decisions that will define what they can expect from you. This is why your first decisions should be measured not only in terms of the specific cases but also in terms of their total impact on the behavior people will expect from you in the future.

It doesn't make it easier that the information you have in your hands during this initial period is limited. Your decision making may be more difficult and you may need to be more conservative and possibly slower and less agile.

Don't waste time. Turn these initial decision-making cases to your advantage.

At each decision-making point, gather the information, outline your choices, and if the information you have is insufficient, trust your instinct, your gut, and make a bold decision.

Let your initial position on an issue "be tough."

If you do not have enough knowledge, if the information you have is insufficient and time is demanding action, then choose to be tough as your initial position. It is always easier to start tough and soften up later than to get tough when you've started out soft.

Willem's Case
Willem van der Wooden
General Manager, Telecommunications, Netherlands

Willem knows that taking a decision with little information always makes managers conservative. He advises the opposite, however. Be tough and send a message.

"I was not more than one month on the job when I was faced with an issue about sexual harassment. A sales representative brought a formal complaint against her sales supervisor. The information came only from one side, with not a lot of evidence.

"We checked the background information, spoke with people from the previous companies that person was working for. Although we got more information that something was going on and all people investigating were feeling uncomfortable with such behavior, we still did not have clear and enough substantiated evidence to support fully a decision.

"I made the decision to fire the person. The decision was tougher than we would take under normal circumstances for the simple reason that I wanted to send a message about compliance and ethics across the company."

Send signals that you expect speed and will not tolerate complacency.

Speed? How can you send a message about "speed"?

Well, one way to do that is by setting stretched deadlines. That way you can achieve results earlier as well as test the level of readiness, flexibility, and speed of your organization.

By applying the same pressure (in terms of deadlines, to use the same example) across the different departments and managers, you will also get an idea of the speed and efficiency among the various departments. You will therefore gain useful benchmarking information about the business readiness across your company.

Don't waste valuable time in getting ready to act. Just do it!

"Aim-FIRE-Ready" versus the normal Ready-Aim-Fire: that's what John Kotter, the world famous change guru says, and the majority of successful managers out there agree with him.

Don't wait for all relevant information and input before you make a decision. Perfect information does not exist and, even if it does, waiting for it will take you out of the game simply by making you too late.

Make sure you are not "firing" alone but that your core management team is participating and leading along with you.

Involving people from different levels in clearing out bottlenecks can be very valuable.

People from lower levels, being closer to the issue than anybody else, can provide more suitable solutions. At the same time they will become motivated simply by being asked to participate. Try it with your team!

Pascal's Case
Pascal Le Graf, General Manager
Telecommunications, USA

When people are hungry for change and you give them the chance, you can perform miracles easily and fast. You have to create the right environment and discussion platform and then let your people run with the project.

Pascal remembers: "I faced a case of having several bottle-necks and well as unclear policies in several areas during one of my marketing and sales assignments with a multinational company.

"While the people were very good functionally, the lack of clear systems and processes slowed them down and created lots of frustration. You could see it in the faces of the people, as what they really wanted to do was to be in front of the customer rather than wasting their time trying to manage the internal procedures monster.

"We brainstormed with participants across hierarchy levels and with representation across departments. We separated the issues according to the importance to the business and the sense of urgency and finally ended up with two types of work streams:

"1. Low-Hanging Fruits.
"These were the short term needs, the issues that required immediate handling and can be addressed now. We addressed bottlenecks related to existing processes and systems. Teams

were asked to provide practical recommendations within two to four weeks.

"2. 'Cobras.'

"These were the thornier issues that could not be immediately solved. Teams were required to meet on a weekly basis and provide recommendations within two to three months. In this framework, we addressed mostly new areas through innovative and out-of-the-box thinking.

"Did it work? You bet it did.

"Participants appreciated the opportunity to participate, to challenge and to execute their own solutions."

"New-Leader Assimilation"

"New Leader Assimilation" is a leadership workshop. It gives the opportunity for your immediate team to get to know you and for you to send out initial messages about your management style and your objectives.

It is also a prime opportunity to clear the air from misunderstandings.

The "New-Leader Assimilation" is rather well known and relatively widely used by several progressive companies and managers.

What does such a session cover?

Like the "Teachable Point of View," it centers around your ideas, your values, and your areas of emotional energy. It is a good idea to share your teachable points of view during your feedback part.

The following steps ensure a successful "New-Leader Assimilation" workshop:

Find the right time for the session

Have this session after you have been in your new role for at least two months. This gives your direct reports enough time to see you in action, to understand your style, and to experience enough examples of your decision making to give you their feedback.

Get an expert to facilitate it

A facilitator other than yourself runs this workshop. You do not attend this part. It helps if the facilitator is not one of your direct reports. An outside expert can listen to your direct reports without any bias, while your direct reports will feel free to offer comments without being afraid of breached confidentiality. The expert can be from outside your company or from another unit within the company. Either way, the more credible he/she is, the more successful the workshop will be.

Facilitator seeks feedback

The facilitator starts the brainstorming session in a structured manner by asking the group to identify their positive and negative impressions of you. If the number of participants is larger than, say, eight or ten people, then it is recommended that participants break out in groups.

It goes without saying that the facilitator does not participate in the brainstorming session and that all information provided by the people is treated as confidential. You are not to know who says what in this meeting.

Debrief session

The group provides feedback, then they take a break. During the break, the facilitator meets with you, summarizes the feedback, and helps you prepare your own feedback to the group on the points raised.

Expect surprises, but focus your feedback on the key items
Do not be surprised if some of the feedback is not what you expect it to be or if it is not fair in your eyes. Some of the comments will be strong, even biased. Receive them calmly and try to address them directly and honestly.

Be humble and appreciative when you give your feedback

Start by thanking the participants for their honesty and comments, emphasizing the importance of this session for you and your relationship with them.

Stay positive, talk softly, and look all of them in their eyes

Cover their concerns. Without being apologetic, show genuine interest in their comments.

At the end, make a "promise list" of items or areas where you agree with them, and promise to pay special attention to this list.

Avoid possible traps

Although such sessions are very helpful and can assure your department about the value you place on the feedback, be alert enough to avoid possible traps.

Some people might see such sessions as perfect opportunities to create negative waves against you and to emphasize your weaknesses and faults instead of your strong points.

If you expect such malicious behavior from one or more of your direct reports, let the facilitator know ahead of time so she/he can manage this discussion accordingly. An experienced facilitator will be able to single out such behavior easily and handle it appropriately, either by filtering the malicious feedback or by managing the discussion flow to give "biased" participants less opportunity to vent their venom.

Takeaways

- Manage others' first impression of you well to create a long lasting, positive image. When you start from 0-base, impressions are always important, but the first ones are the most important.

- Communicate your values and ideas right from the start, make yourself predictable, make your style known, and gain time and leadership points.

- Provide formal and informal opportunities for your people to critique you and learn what they think about you. Give them opportunities to speak up.

- Take the feedback your direct reports give you with a smile. Show genuine interest, don't reply back, don't try to justify, don't try to explain. Just shut up and listen.

Now that you know how to make a good start, let's change gears towards strategy. Chapter Seven shows you how you can make strategy executional.

7

If you are a believer in the concept of "managing from 20,000 feet," be careful.

The higher you believe you are managing from, the harder the impact of your fall will be.

Link Strategy to Execution to Achieve Superior Performance

The European Management Center in Brussels gives some of the best definitions on strategy, from contemporary ones like "strategy is the positioning of an organization within its competitive framework" to more theoretic but still realistic ones such as "strategy is the art of appearing consistently lucky."

For some industries, the definition becomes even more straightforward, such as the "Rule of Ten Percent" that the Japanese adopted when competing against Intel in the memory chip business. Their strategy of dropping prices ten percent whenever Intel brought out a new chip allowed the Japanese to stay in the competitive game while at the same time they were working hard on the innovation front until they were able to catch up with the technological advancement.

Many general managers can develop strategy.

Even more can execute strategy extremely well.

However, the general managers who can make the link between the two are the rare ones, the ones that are born to lead and destined to succeed.

Making the link from strategy to execution is one of the most challenging and critical jobs of the general manager.

From PowerPoint® presentations to rolled-up sleeves is quite a distance. It takes a special kind of manager: the bound-to-succeed one!

In this chapter, you will learn how to manage strategy.

You will be exposed to concepts and systems to help you set strategy up, align it, communicate it, and operationalize it.

A better link between strategy and execution creates higher levels of commitment, personal ownership, and momentum. It makes roles in the organization clearer and more tightly connected.

Simplify Strategy and Increase Employee Understanding and Alignment toward Company Goals

Do all employees know what the company strategy is?

Do the various levels of the organization share the same understanding of the strategy?

Simplify strategy enough so it can be embedded in the minds and hearts of the people in the organization, throughout management, and down to the field- and floor-based employees.

Simplification increases horizontal and vertical understanding, as well as belief in and commitment to strategy. The general manager needs to make the strategy easy to understand for his own unit.

We have all been in management strategy meetings where managers leave the meeting room more confused than they had been before the meeting.

I am referring to the meetings where 40 to 100 managers are assembled in a hotel for a couple of days, bombarded with tons of PowerPoint® slides, and then sent back home, along with a 50-page booklet to share with their units.

How can you simplify strategy?

Simplify it by using a one-pager covering:

- • the overall goal of the company expressed by the strategy

- the main strategy parameters, the milestones, timelines, and key players

- What the strategy means for your unit and what is expected from your people

  - What targets are affected?
  - What timelines apply?
  - How is the allocation of resources impacted?

- • Where each person fits in the strategy

- What it will look like at the end of the journey, showing them the before and the after.

- What they will get out of it—company strength, incentives, positioning, etc.

The less paper or fewer slides you use, the more successful simplifying your strategy will be.

The more complicated and stretched the strategy, the simpler and leaner the message communicating should be.

The Author's Case
The Author, Healthcare
Paris, France

I am a firm believer in oversimplification as well as over-communication of strategy. You can never over-convince and over-align, and even if you do, it is very positive as it means that you are closer to "over-achieving.

In a recent strategy change for Bristol-Myers Squibb, business units around the world were required to adjust their models and structure.

In spite of the aggressive strategy, tough timelines, and gifted people in charge, how it was to be applied across the world depended on the global portfolio alignment, or lack of which was the case here. The smaller the portfolio link, the bigger the change required in the model, as was the case in METRA (Middle East, Eastern Europe, Turkey, Africa) that I was managing at the time.

To simplify it, I created the "remodeling" concept: a seven-phase approach to communicating the strategy, making it applicable to our unit, and monitoring its execution...all in a single page!

This one-pager was the main way we communicated our strategy. It was shown across a two-year period over 100 times across 20 or more countries.

Throughout the remodeling period of three years, in every meeting I attended, I asked if anyone among the participants had not seen this page.

Even if only one person said no, I would take ten minutes to go through it for everybody.

Do you think my message was strong enough?

Make Strategy Easy to Execute and Improve Commitment and Productivity

MAKING STRATEGY EXECUTIONAL

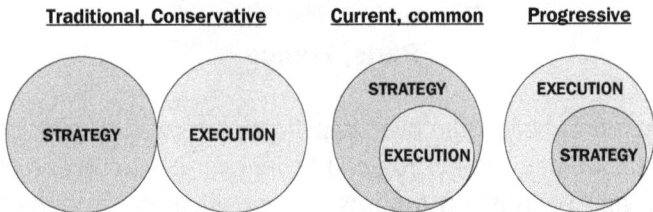

Traditional, Conservative   Current, common   Progressive

STRATEGY   EXECUTION   STRATEGY / EXECUTION   EXECUTION / STRATEGY

Do you believe that some people should get paid only to "strategize" while others should only execute?

Are you one of these managers who believe in managing from 20,000 feet?

If so, be careful! The higher you believe you are managing from, the harder the impact will be when you fall.

How do traditional managers link strategy and execution?

Traditionally, managers separate strategy from execution, making a very weak link between the two.

They see them as different parts that touch each other only at the one point when they move from ideas to tasks.

Such a model is conservative and risky. It cannot achieve the alignment between strategy and execution necessary for maximal performance.

The level of collaboration is compromised, taking the level of performance down with it.

How do most contemporary companies view strategy and execution?

Most companies view execution as part of strategy, as its operational or executional arm. Such models have been and can still be successful but not sustainable for the longer term. As the environment changes, smart companies change their approach to strategy accordingly.

Viewing execution as an arm to strategy only is a reflection of the recent past where markets and industries were characterized by growth. This is how most markets, both as industries and as geographies, were until the late '90s.

Strategies were geared towards either achieving a higher rate of growth or a bigger piece of a growing segment. Companies were focused on strategy and not execution simply because all strategies seemed to be working.

Strategizing within that environment can be more futuristic, more theoretical, more daring and less executional, simply because results are functions of positive market factors and not only company efforts.

With the top line being healthy, companies felt more comfortable in changing strategy, following expansion strategies, growing structures, taking risks.

Obviously, smarter companies got a bigger piece of the pie, but everybody had a good chance of succeeding.

If your company still operates in such an environment, you are in good shape...at least for now

But the business world has changed for most companies, industries, and markets. Growth does not come easy, and when it does come, it comes at a higher cost. Growth parameters such as product innovation, new market entries, and price inelasticity are hard to find, extremely difficult to sustain, and very costly.

As if those trends were not bad enough, new "constraints" came into place, such as compliance on ethics and business practices, that have changed the performance map drastically.

Why do I see better business ethics and practices as "constraints"? Because they are! The bad practices of some have slowed down markets, reduced the value of companies, and created fear across industries and companies.

Some people say that for the longer term, conformity to ethics will become a competitive advantage. I seriously doubt it. I believe that companies will adjust quicker and improve deeper and faster before anyone creates a competitive advantage in this area.

I also believe that companies will lose competitive edge, as most will focus on compliance and process while they become risk-averse. They will become focused more internally and less towards the customer.

How do progressive leaders manage strategy and execution?

Progressive leaders focus on execution. They make execution the centerpiece of efforts and strategy a part of it.

Don't misunderstand the concept. Strategy has been, is, and will be important, but once it is set, engraved, communicated, and owned, then execution takes over.

Execution becomes broader than implementation of strategy. Execution includes parts of the main strategies horizontally and vertically within each activity.

So be involved in all matters of strategy and execution through the platform you have created.

Align targets to reflect the overall goals, set the right milestones, align resources behind it, and measure performance appropriately to increase accountability and monitor work output.

"If we continue emphasizing strategy over execution, all we will have at the end is strategy" (Peter Dolan, ex-C.E.O., Bristol-Myers Squibb Company).

Show clearly how individuals' roles fit into the strategy, what is expected of them, and why their roles are important.

> Back in 1966, three years before the first person stepped on the moon, a survey was conducted at NASA to see the level of commitment to the vision, to the goal.
>
> The most astounding reply came from an older member of the cleaning staff who was sweeping the floor at the time of the interview.
>
> When asked what his role at NASA was, he stood straight up and with all the pride that a sixty-year-old, tired body could handle, said: "My role is very clear I help put a man on the moon, Sir!"

Can you think of a more simplified strategy?

Can you think of a better linkage between each person's role and strategy?

Was there a chance this mega-NASA project would fail?

Institutionalize Strategy and Build Personal Employee Ownership and Trust

For strategy to be successful and sustained for the long run, it must become institutionalized.

Institutionalized strategies are the ones that are so well embedded in the company culture that they become integral parts of the management systems and processes. Institutionalized strategies are communicated loudly and consistently in order to build trust in them.

"If you are able to institutionalize trust, you have achieved the maximum in strategizing. Strategy will be strong and will continue even when the founders of strategy depart."

How do you institutionalize a strategy?

First, you create deeply rooted alignments and commitments to the strategy across management layers:

- Involve key people early through their participation in the strategic planning or budgeting process.
- Choose carefully who participates in each part of the process. Ensure that each participant's role fits what they do on a daily basis.

  Prevent people from viewing their participation in strategy management as a theoretical job which they exercise in meetings and then go back to doing things the old way or differently when they return to their office or daily tasks. There must be a strong link to what people do on a daily basis and to what strategy dictates everybody should be doing.

- Establish management forums where strategy is established and monitored (see "The Strategy Brain Workshop," p. 89).

  Communicate the outcomes of these forums among all employees, adjusting the content to fit each audience but giving the same consistent message.

Jim's Case
Jim Atkinson, Director
Healthcare, Nyon, Switzerland

Jim reminds us that it always pays to involve more experienced people when implementing new strategies. Smart and committed managers can help new leaders and new strategies achieve maximum results more quickly. You have to be open to listen and adjust as well as them.

"Although the recent performance of the emerging markets organization I had just taken over was not good, they had been a successful unit in the past and had a lot of experience in often-difficult markets. They had just lost their way and were regarded as something of a misfit organization that was little understood.

"I had been the European finance director, and this was my first job on the commercial side. I knew that I had a lot to learn and that I would have to work hard at getting the organization's respect.

"Although I made it clear through various actions that things weren't going to stay the same, I tried hard to listen to the experienced team members and respect their inputs, and didn't come in as though I knew all the answers.

"Things took a while to turn around, but the approach worked.

"By trying to understand the staff and being willing to change myself, I got the respect of the team."

Second, set milestones for institutionalizing each part of the strategy process. Then ensure that you achieve each single milestone by:

- Adjusting the level of urgency and focus towards the main milestones.

- Reallocating resources as necessary to increase the probability of hitting the milestones.

- Adjusting targets, strategy, and information flow if you see that a milestone will not be achieved. That way, you keep the momentum strong in spite of the lost milestone. You should feel rather comfortable about losing some battles as long as you win the important ones and win the war. If you move from battle to battle without losing a single one, you have not taken enough risks.

    Celebrating the accomplishment of each milestone by giving appropriate acknowledgment to key individual contributors and teams and pointing out how this milestone fits into the longer-term strategy

Being tough in criticizing underachievement and lower-than-expected execution.

Third, increase ownership through the right communication, meaning the right frequency and depth of contact to ensure commitment, alignment, and consistency of execution. Here are some hints:

- Always use consistent terminology. Avoid negative and passive terms and words that imply the status quo. Avoid terms like "maintain," "continue," and "keep." Use terminology that applies to war or games rules, like: "attack," "defend," "again," "ground," "create momentum," "aggressive," "stretched," and "realistic."

- Plan your frequency of communication well and follow it religiously. Do not assume that because the message is well heard and understood at your level and above, all layers below you have the same understanding and commitment.

- Ensure the support of sponsors, meaning your own boss and the chosen key executives above you. The messages that sponsors send to your people must reinforce yours in their consistency and strength. It is the job of the general manager to ask or remind his boss and other executives to include specific messages about the efforts you are making in your unit to foster the disciplined execution of the strategy. Do not assume that your boss will know when and what to say on his/her own.

Appivita, a Greece-based international cosmetics company is such an example. As their product concept has been built on nature-found flora, Appivita's management guard their visionary concept so tightly that it is evident in each one of their activities, from the raw material used all the way to the selection of business partners and promotional practices.

For example, they will only hire people who know nature and respect their business concept. They partner with suppliers and others only if they adhere to these high expectations.

Try to talk to its owners for five minutes and count the number of times you will hear the words "nature," "honey," "bees," "values," "respect."

Some successful companies achieve high levels of linkage between strategy and execution because they take it further; they make a condition of doing business.

Does such a strategy have a cost? Surely it does, usually in terms of lost opportunities or margin, but such longer-term resilience to values and ethics can only enhance brand and company equity.

The Strategy Brain Workshop—A Winning System to Manage Strategy

The Strategy Brain Workshop is a system that helps you set strategy, align the team behind it, and monitor its implementation.

The Strategy Brain Workshop is a two-day meeting where the top twenty or so managers of your business unit or company:

- analyze the expectations by top management for the period under review.

- analyze how the company currently measures up in meeting these objectives.

- prioritize all key projects and define the milestones to be achieved.

How does "The Strategy Brain Workshop" work?

- The team identifies the critical success factors, or the issues and opportunities which you need to deal with effectively if you want to achieve your objectives.

  Depending on the industry, critical success factors can vary, but the general categories include:

  a. Performance (new product launches, investment plans
  b. Systems (inventory management, production efficiencies,

etc.)

    c. People (incentive plans, retention plans, etc.)
    d. External environment (government measures, intellectual property protection, etc.)

- Well-selected subgroups list, prioritize, and assign leaders to each project that addresses the critical success factors.

- Optimal prioritization assumes that no more than twenty percent of all projects are categorized as priority "A," no more than thirty percent as priority "B" and all the rest as priority "C."

- Obtain the agreement and commitment of all in the final project list, and have leaders prepare a one-page project outline for each project.

- Set up and have all team members commit to the deliverables for each project.

- Announce the date of the next Strategy Brain Workshop meeting. Such meetings usually should take place two or three times per year.

- During mid-year progress reviews or in Strategy Brain Workshop meetings, cast your opinion through voting on each project's progress (even electronically to ensure transparency) and make adjustments. These adjustments may include: changes in the prioritization of projects, changes of leaders who are not keeping up with expectations, and recalibration of milestones.

This meeting should take place outside the company offices and possibly in a different city or country to take advantage of the great opportunity it presents for team-building.

A human resources manager can organize it, but the occasional participation of outside consultants or facilitators is encouraged.

A facilitator increases efficiency by keeping things focused on the strategy and not project details, which can only take the meeting off track.

The Strategy Brain Workshop concept is similar to the 'Balanced Scorecard" model, developed by Robert Kaplan and David Norton.

Strategist Projects
GROUP: PERFORMANCE

Priority	Project Name	Marketing	Sales	Human Resources	Production	Qtr 1	Qtr 2	Qtr 3	Qtr 4	Project Leader
A	Product X launch	x	x							S Allen
A	New production line opening				x					W Billington
A	Joint-venture establishment in India	x			x					D Barnes
B	Rewards & Recognition Initiative launch			x						A Abdalla
B	Advertising agency pitchings	x								J Curtis
C	Rep's new training module		x	x						A Morales
C	Expansion of sales force in product Y		x							H Patel
C	Market research on market B		x							J Vasquez
C	Cost-saving Initiative				x					W Kim
C	Leadership program at Columbia	x								J Lohre

Project start-up time
Project duration

It is a management concept that helps managers at all levels prioritize and monitor performance.

Takeaways

- Oversimplify strategy to the degree that the security guard or the telephone operator can describe it in thirty seconds. The less paper or fewer slides you use to describe strategy, the more easily it can be communicated and committed to.

- You will have achieved the perfect link of strategy and execution when every employee can describe how their role fits into the company strategy and what their personal contribution towards achieving the strategic company goals will be.

- Don't start promoting the new strategy to people in lower levels before you get the blessing of the people above you.

- Systems create discipline, and discipline creates trust. Trust in business is not a personal thing only. For trust to be long-lived it needs to be incorporated in policies, processes, and systems.

You now know that linking strategy to execution increases organizational performance and evolves your organization.

Evolution is change, and in Chapter Eight you will unravel this important area through systems for understanding what needs to be changed and then preparing for it.

8

Once in a while we need to take a leap off *a* cliff.
Just so we can feel the blood running in our veins.

Successful Change:
First Understand It!

Why change anything anyway? Is there a need for change in the company?

These are fair questions. After all, we should not be changing just for the sake of it. There must be something in change that demonstrates a benefit, an improvement of some sort, versus the current situation.

To maximize the effect of change, the costs of the change and, most importantly, the benefits of the change must be measurable, quantifiable, comparable, and visible.

In this chapter, you will learn why the best change is the one that becomes part of routine and not simply a strategic choice or option.

You will see why to "stand still" or to "keep the status quo" cannot be strategy and that the change that you decide to implement on your own is the most effective type of change.

So What Is Change?

Change is evolution
Successful change is an ongoing, continuous process of evolvement. Substantial improvement can come through change that alters rigid beliefs or practices.

Ideal organizations incorporate change in their daily life simply as part of routine.

It's a paradox, isn't it? The more routine change becomes, the more evolutionary it will be.

When this evolutionary process takes place, the organization will jump way ahead of the competition.

Jim Atkinson of Beckman Coulter International adds that although this is almost always true for the long term, in the short term each wave of change needs to be monitored closely, because it may create a gap in our competitive position.

Change is identical to survival

Have your heard these statements before:

"Our target is to maintain the current market share."
"Our strategy is to keep the same level of performance."

Statements that use words like "maintain," "keep," and "preserve" cannot be strategic. They contain a conservatism, a lack of innovation, an aversion to risk, and a pathetic attitude.

The competitive environment is getting so tough that you cannot afford to stand still.

Choose to move ahead, to grow. You can also choose to decline (managing decline can be a beautiful business, I assure you!) but to stand still should not be one of your options in the cockpit.

Standing still is a failure strategy.

Change is leadership

There isn't a single leader who did not make change the heart of his efforts.

There isn't a single leader who doesn't have "change" written on his forehead.

It's that simple, ladies and gentlemen. That simple!

Change is challenge

Do you work in a complacent organization?

Do you want change to be sustained, deep and for the long term?

Is the informal definition of culture in your company, "the way we do things around here"?

Then you have your work cut out for you.

Start challenging!

Challenge the status quo and conventional thinking.

Challenge continuously, decreasing the things you and the people around you consider to be normal and accepted parts of the environment.

Challenge yourself and others!

Dennis' Case
Dennis Chia, General Manager
Healthcare, Asia

Dennis implemented change successfully by selecting carefully the areas he needed to challenge and then focusing on those areas. Everything else fell into place afterwards.

"I was appointed general manager of Taiwan in July 2002. Before I left for Taipei, the parting message from my area vice president was pretty straightforward. 'The business there is dying [for the last 3 years]. We want you to fix it!' When I got there, these were my observations:

"The key managers were very experienced, which was good.

"The objective was to increase sales of promoted brands. There appeared to be adequate resources allocated behind these brands. Also good.

"Despite the above, overall sales were below expectation. That was not good!

"*So what needed fixing?*

"It wasn't too long before I realized that the sales team was not organized to focus on the key brands. Not enough focus on the brands of the future. They seemed to be selling a little bit of everything.

"The issues were:

- The sales representative incentive was based on total sales, a single number, not on the performance of each key brand.
- The sales director was protecting his turf. Switching to product lines would have meant moving to a business unit model, which meant this guy would lose his number-two position in the organization behind the general manager.
- The front line sales managers wanted more products so that they could trade off prices across products to make their customers happy.
- It was very difficult to have well-trained representatives, as they were responsible for too many products.

"Clearly the challenge was a fundamental one.

"I reorganized the model from line management to business units focusing on the key brands, created smaller but focused sales teams, and changed the incentive plans to tie them to performance on the key brands.

"The sales director was convinced to give up his turf, but he eventually left the company.

"The results of this change were spectacular. A year later, total sales and sales of key brands exceeded expectations."

Change is about "building commitment into something new"

This is the most important definition of change.

To understand it better and to make it actionable, let's break down the important words: "building," "commitment," and "new."

- **Building:** Building will not happen overnight. It will take timed effort. It will take persistence and determination in order to change deeply rooted beliefs, practices, and habits.

  It will take trial and error, over and over again, gradually building up a momentum, making change take place and stick for the long term.

- **Commitment:** We are not talking about getting people to simply say, "I like your idea." We are not looking for affecting things at the surface.

  We are looking for commitment, which means change in behavior or beliefs.

  How do we achieve that?

  Create a reason *why* change is needed. Show everyone that there is something good at the end of the tunnel.

  Identify the advantages of change, measure them, and communicate them once they have been achieved. You will build momentum and belief in change as you move along.

  People are more likely to agree to participate in a change if at least two of the following conditions are met:

  - The results are visible, easily imagined, or attainable and, preferably, measurable.

  - They see personal reward for them at the end of this process or even during the process. This can vary from overall job security and working for a better-performing company up to awards, acknowledgment for team, or personal participation in the successful change process.

  - They see short-term results from their efforts while they work toward longer-term benefits at the end of the change process.

- **Something New:** Most people are afraid of anything new, unless it is a salary increase!

  This is natural and human. People who are asked to participate in a change process will not join easily.

For most people it is actually quite simple: "I like things the way they are. If I wanted something else, I would not be here in the first place."

When you ask people with this attitude not just to change but also to work for it, you have your work cut out.

You need to define this "something new," to make it visible. Start by creating a small group who will buy into this "something new" and then, gradually, bring more people into the game, expanding your team.

Types of Change

Is your headquarters asking you to apply change in your organization as part of a wider company strategy?

Do you have deep and serious issues that are crying out for change?

Do you believe that you need to lead change proactively, not because it is needed now but because it is indispensable to the future success of your unit?

There are different types of change that need to be applied, depending on the situation on hand.

Depending on the need for change, it can be a smooth and almost unfelt evolutionary process or it can be an abrupt, radical transformation.

Who will decide whether your organization needs change?

Who will decide what type of change is more appropriate? Who will choose the implementation framework?

Let's look into the main types of change and the strategic options for ensuring deep and sustainable success:

"Dictated Change"

This is a change you make to some part of your organization as part of a global or regional initiative, perhaps specifically for your unit but, in all cases, one that is dictated by others. Usually those "others" are none other than headquarters.

There are cases where change is forced by employees (such as unions) or government regulation, but because these are the minority of cases, they will not be part of our focus.

It is headquarters that will decide on smaller or larger changes in investment or structure and then ask you to "simply do it." They can ask directly through face-to-face meetings or indirectly through announcements by a senior leader from management. Headquarters may be open to comments or criticism or they may simply dictate it by providing a description of the outcome (the objective, or how they want things to look like after the change is implemented).

Mergers and acquisitions are examples of non-negotiable types of change. They come without much notice and require full compliance. The centralization or decentralization of functions is another example.

Jim Atkinson, Beckman Coulter International SA, cautions that although dictated change can become more challenging when it relates to centralization and decentralization models, it is still the easier level of change to apply since:

- Your people will accept easily change when it is part of a larger regional or global initiative.

- People will understand and digest change faster when they see their colleagues in other business units and functions also changing.

- Your direct reports will have a good reason to explain the need for change to their own people in their respective departments.

- The methodology and implementation framework is usually quite well defined and, in most cases, prepared almost entirely, in detail, by headquarters.

Your results will be benchmarked against those of similar business units within your company. Grab this opportunity to distinguish and enhance your image and career.

Elena's Case
Elena Trenton, Regional Head
Healthcare, USA

Elena advises you to take the opportunity of dictated change, perform at your best, and watch your image as a change agent move your career higher.

"When I was heading the Over-the-Counter Division (OTC) for Southern Europe, Mideast, and Asia, I was lucky enough to be selected as the leader of a major transformation process. Until that time, the OTC Divisions in the company were run independently from the core, purely pharmaceutical, part of the company. That required different reporting, supporting, and financial structures.

"I was nominated as the person to integrate the OTC Divisions into the main pharmaceutical company. It was, in a way, an internal, friendly type of acquisition.

"I was given the authority to evaluate what type of consolidation process was required, what would be the cost and benefit relationship, and how the impact would look in terms of numbers.

"The funny part was that I was coming from the part of the business that was being consolidated, which made things more challenging for me but also more interesting and rewarding in terms of learning and the satisfaction of having done the 'unusual.'

"It was a successful project, implemented across a geographical span of over twenty countries, different old models, and across various cultures.

"Did it help my career? You bet it did. Several years after, my image as an effective change agent continues to help my career."

How can you implement dictated change effectively?

- Clarify early on exactly what management is looking for. Identify the objectives and align their prioritization with your management ones.

- Believe in it yourself. Become a master of the change plan. Talk to people who have worked on the change concept, and talk to critics of it. Consult with change experts from within your company and outside. Become an expert in communicating change and make execution easier.

- Set a timetable that allows you to do a quality job and meet the expectations of your management. If the project is done across the company, make sure that you set tight-enough deadlines to make your progress faster and better when compared to the other units.

- Provide frequent progress updates to the key stakeholders. Keep management informed in a timely and proactive manner. Don't surprise them.

- Talk to the change agents below you directly and clearly. Do not allow room for debate on *what* will be done, as this might compromise the objectives. On the other hand, be open, listen, and use others' ideas about *how* to execute more effectively. Include their ideas about how to implement change to generate higher participation and commitment by your people and improve the success of the change.

- Be personally accountable for the change. "It is a top-management decision. What can I do?" is the wrong position to take. Under no circumstances should you blame headquarters for change. Yes, it can and should be presented as part of a company-wide initiative. Yes, it should be emphasized in cases where the negotiation is tough. But under no circumstances should it be used as the single reason for the change.

    If you claim that headquarters has decided the change and you are simply implementing it, then you will appear weak, people will lose trust in you as well as headquarters, and you will eventually fail.

"Needed Change"
Needed change is usually an internal change within the division or company you are personally managing.

When is that?

Needed change is usually called for when things are not going well, when an internal crisis takes place, or when productivity or some other measure significantly fails to meet expectations.

How should you approach it?

Welcome such type of change and lead your organization toward it. *Here are some reasons why:*

- Things are in bad shape and need to be fixed. Someone needs to step in and champion the change. Situations like this are great opportunities for new general managers. Hopefully you are lucky enough (!) to take over from someone who has left some problems that need to be and can be fixed rather easily.

- Show what you can do very quickly. In most cases of needed change, the problem is evident. The "bleeding" is hurting productivity and morale. What a great chance for you to win fans and followers right from the start! Handling this type of challenge quickly and successfully will help you gain credibility from headquarters as well.

- The problems needing change are easy to spot and, in most cases, easy to solve. When you solve them, don't forget to celebrate the change with your team, rewarding them for their contribution and creating momentum. Don't forget to also communicate your success to management. This will demonstrate your initiative and results orientation, right from the outset of your assignment.

"Chosen Change"

Do you want to go to the top quicker? Then apply "chosen change"!

With chosen change, no one is dictating that you change anything! Furthermore, no obvious need necessitates the change!

It is your choice. You are choosing to change because you want to achieve higher performance faster, because you want to be ahead of others, and because you are visionary.

This is by far the most challenging and most difficult change to apply, but it also the most rewarding and possibly enjoyable type of change to make.

This is the change that distinguishes great leaders from good managers.

Why such change should take place

• Choose to change and be in front of the wave, steer its direction, set its pace and its strength.

• Choose to change because you want to be in charge of your destiny. Do it before others come and dictate it to you.

Tony Hooper, President of U.S. Medicines for Bristol-Myers Squibb Company, describes change in terms of a wave: "By following change you are behind the wave and trying to keep up with it. By being on top of the wave you are keeping pace with it. But by being ahead of the wave you are proactively and pre-emptively managing the wave." It is this last part, being ahead of the wave, that makes this type of change the most important one.

• Choose to change because you are a far-sighted leader, one of the small minority of great individuals who are striving to fight now in order to build a better future. Build for the long term now while hitting the short-term targets.

Characteristics of "Chosen Change"

• It is the toughest type of change since people will definitely and naturally resist it more than they would a dictated or needed change.

• It is proactive in nature. A small group of people leads it while others are mostly reluctant to participate, especially if they do not see the benefit in the short run.

- It must have the support of a strong sponsor. This could be your boss or managers higher up in the organization who back you up when things start getting tough.

- The pace of change needs to be set according to the size of the battle. The bigger the battle, the more well prepared and cautious your pace should be.

If you work in a visionary company where change and innovation is part of the culture, then things will be easier, regardless of whether the change is dictated, needed, or chosen.

Takeaways

- Make change routine, not a strategic choice. When change is an option, it means there are alternatives. But, there should not be alternatives once change is chosen, at least not for organizations that want to survive and dominate.

- Don't choose to "stand still" or to "keep the status quo" as your strategy. These are failure strategies for your organization, and you will go down with them.

- If you don't face resistance to change, double-check. Maybe you are not changing fast and deeply enough.

- Don't wait for others to dictate change to you. Choose to change and increase your control over your staff's minds, hearts, and careers...and yours!

As you have seen in this chapter, change is not an option; the more proactively you change your organization, the higher you will go. The next chapter shows you how to engage your organization behind change and implement it successfully.

9

Some managers breathe strategy. Other managers breathe survival.

The third kind breathes strategy or survival according to which way the wind is blowing. Watch out for the third kind.

Change:
Implement It Successfully

How do you implement successful change? Is there a one-size-fits-all formula that you can use, or is it more complicated than that? Are you going to apply change alone, or should you have a team working with you?

Learn how to apply successful change and affect performance and momentum.

To do this you need to identify the degree of change needed and the time and effort required to implement the change successfully. Then you need to put a strong team behind it.

What system are we talking about?
How about a winning system? A system that is flexible, adjustable, and expandable for each specific change depends on:

- The difficulty of achieving each change objective.

  - Is it easy to apply? Then it can be a quick fix.

  - Is it a deep change? Then you are looking for a different set of tactics.

- The commitment of the change agents to the objective at hand. The higher the commitment, the quicker and more promising the change will be.

- The depth and talent of the change-team members. The lower the talent, the longer it will take to bring about successful change.

"Change" Strategies for Quick Fixes

Is the bottleneck or issue requiring change easily identifiable? Is it easy to put a plan in place?

Are you and your team ready to implement it?

If the answers to the above questions are yes, then you have to make a "quick fix" type of change.

First, look around and identify what decreases speed, takes away productivity, or increases your idle capacity.

Search for the bottlenecks that limit performance and clear them out.

Here are two systems you can use to apply quick change:

System: The "Heartbeat Check"

Choose the most important operational charts and do a quick "heartbeat check" on your operational model. Examples of such charts are inventories, manufacturing/sourcing delays, customer-returns ratios, and sales-forecasting accuracy, as well as charts devoted to talent management such as promotion history, career planning charts, and rewards and recognition tracking.

Take a look at these reports with the assistance of your finance or operations head and identify the black or grey areas which need to be addressed.

System: "Low-Hanging Fruits"

This system pinpoints issues that can be identified and improved without much effort.

What are some examples of "low-hanging fruits"? *Communication and reporting, travel policies, invoicing delays, collections delays, and sales-force-request process time.*

How do you go about it?
First, identify the problem areas.

Create small, agile task forces and have them brainstorm on processes, reports, etc. Ask each task force to come up with a list of hurdles that can be overcome quickly.

Second, prioritize the areas to be fixed according to how much of a bottleneck they represent and how little it takes to solve them. Projects that require a longer time to fix are out of the scope of this study and put under the "systems" approach explained in the previous chapter.

If you don't have the expertise in-house to fix some issues, hire from outside on an assignment basis. It will cost you very little and, in addition to clearing a bottleneck or two, it will keep your organization focused on your main business priorities.

Don't get carried away. There is a limit to how much "low-hanging fruits" you can manage at a given time. Overemphasis on too many low-hanging fruits or for too long a period of time defeats the purpose of having quick change and takes your eyes away from your main priorities.

The Author
General Manager
Healthcare, Asia

"I am living proof that low-hanging fruits need to be identified and addressed quickly; otherwise, this can end up being an endless exercise, compromising objective-attainment and possibly boring people in the process.

"It was back in 2000. I was the general manager of Thailand when I was given the additional responsibility of managing the OTC (over-the-counter medicines) business for Australasia and the Mideast.

"Full of excitement, I made my plans and moved on to manage the business across twenty-some countries.

"Boy, I had a great plan. I prioritized the markets in layers according to the market's size and potential, got corporate approval and full support, and I went ahead, making life difficult for the top-layer countries.

"What did I do wrong?

"Well, without much taking into account the fact that each country head had his/her own priorities and objectives, I marched on and created task forces across countries, across brands, across layers, across everything.

"Was I busy? Yes.

"Was I getting results? Well, it seemed so, mainly because I was pushing too hard and because I was doing some of the work myself for the slower-responding countries.

"I had simply over-expanded myself and the job profile too quickly, into too many areas, and was going directly towards failure or a revolt by the management in these countries.

"Thankfully, one of the country heads and a good colleague, Y.L. Liew (currently regional vice president for Diethelm in Asia), talked to me, and I adjusted the speed to the pace of the local operations."

Change Strategies For Major Change

What is Major Change?

Major change refers to something that drastically alters the way we think and do things. It is deep and vast change that may be dictated by management and/or may be needed to take place internally, and/or may be chosen by you.

Is major change difficult to apply?

You bet!

Major change is neither easily anticipated by employees nor welcomed by the majority of them.

It creates distress and discomfort for most people, especially in the early stages when people do not fully understand the reason for change, their roles within it, or how the final outcome will affect them.

What makes it even more difficult is that the benefits from a major change are not quickly seen. It will take time and require extra effort from you to keep the focus and commitment high until the benefits become visible.

What are some examples of "Major Change"?

- *Management team reshuffling:* Change of memberships or the roles of current members or the addition of new members to the team.

- *Cultural change:* Change in old habits and beliefs, change of incentive and rewards systems, changes to succession plan assumptions, or drastic changes in personnel.

- *Major process and systems change:* Compliance-program implementation that alters the competitive framework or changes performance standards.

- *Centralization of power* into a few people at the higher end of hierarchy.

- Any combination of the above.

Dennis' Case
Dennis Chia, General Manager
Healthcare, Asia

Dennis is a firm believer in the change-team concept, but he insists that you need to choose the right people to participate, show them the way to apply change, and guide them through it.

"Your first three months on the job are like the first trimester of a pregnancy. There are many uncertainties. Your organization expects changes. You are not sure how they will respond to your leadership.

"I usually establish a 'lead team.' I pick the best and brightest from all levels and brainstorm on real-time issues and come up with solutions to solve them.

"I facilitate and observe the group dynamics. In such forums, you will be able to observe who are leaders and the followers. Not all power coalitions will support you. You need to determine the influential ones within and work on them accordingly.

"It is useful to establish a feedback mechanism either through your HR department or someone in whom you can develop trust quickly. I spend lots of time coaching one-on-one, facilitating team meetings on a regular basis. There are always cliques in your organization. It is useful to identify the coalition of power. If they are allied to you, then it is more likely that you can effect changes quickly and successfully.

"Put good people behind opportunities to achieve results.

"Success breeds success, and you build the team's confidence in you quickly."

Building a Change Team

For change to be planned well, implemented well, and sustained for the long term, you need to build a change team. This is a group of people who will buy in early, support you in your ideas, and become ambassadors in spreading them throughout the organization.

The risks of choosing the wrong people for the change team are delays, non-alignment, problems with the allocation of workload, and the overall dilution of your effectiveness.

How do you choose the right change-team members?

Regardless of the change you are aiming for, several common characteristics help you screen and qualify people to be included in the change team:

- *Their relation to the change area and their expertise in the change subject.* It would be fruitless and counter-productive to have a room full of people who can only offer humble, general opinions about what needs to be done but who have little to do with the technicalities of the planning and implementation stages.

- *Their track record or desire to participate in change.* Sometimes you can simply see in the eyes of the people whether they will be willing to jump on an initiative.

- Their previous participation in one or more of the quick-fix initiatives which you have put into place in the recent past. The level of involvement in a "quick fix" can qualify or disqualify a change task-force candidate.

- Smart and able people who, for whatever reason, have been neglected from the previous management make good candidates. They will be looking forward to the opportunity to prove a thing or two.

- *Their ability to influence others in the organization.* People with high credibility and network connections in the company will help you get by quicker than other departments.

- *People who come from different levels in the hierarchy* will make sure that views are mixed and heard across organizational layers.

How do you maximize the effectiveness of a change team?

- *Identify the personal objectives that each change-team member has for participating in the change effort.* What do they expect to gain from being involved in this change process? What is in it for them?

- *Include "drivers"—people who can lead and challenge.* Complement them with a good number of "followers"—people who follow directions and implement flawlessly.

- *Keep the change team small.* At the initial stages of the change, the team should be small in number. A team of five to ten people is optimal. A larger number of participants turns the change team into a forum and limits its effectiveness.

- *Expand the number of change-team members when you have built a good base in your change efforts.* This is usually when you have accomplished some early wins and you want to expand change across organizational layers faster.

- *Involve your direct reports.* This is the most critical line of managers to win and the most resistant one. Remember, they represent the status quo that you are there to change!

Manage the Speed of Change and Gain Efficiency in Change-Implementation

Speed is a key component of a successful change. It leads to quicker decisions and limits the time for resistance to change to build up.

Going fast, however, can have drawbacks. It can lead to wrong decisions, because your information and analysis will be limited.

Finding the balance between the drawbacks and benefits is key. It is related to the pressure you are under to change.

Roland's Case
Roland Bruhin, Regional Director
Asia North, Logistics, Hong Kong

Roland is a firm believer that in crisis situations, speed is important, but not at any cost. Depending on the circumstances, however, balancing speed allows for a better and broader perspective and assessment of the overall situation.

"It was back in July 1997 when I was the general manager of our subsidiary in Thailand.

"The Asian crisis had just begun, with Thailand being forced to devalue the Thai Baht, which in turn went into freefall, dragging down other Asian economies and their currencies. I had just taken over as managing director of this company.

"The company had been one hundred percent financed in American dollars. The organization was focused on sales, and the word, 'collection,' was considered almost a dirty word. Control processes were extremely weak or non-existent. In the boom years preceding, the company got away with it; with a fundamentally changed economic environment where most corporations were cash-strapped, the chickens came home to roost.

"The senior management team consisted of mid-thirties, ambitious Thai people who had grown up in the boom era. There was no concept whatsoever to cope with the demands of such an extreme situation.

"Nevertheless, by September we were among the first companies to restructure and to downsize, reducing the head count by twenty-five percent. While we were quick to act, the gravity of the situation necessitated another cut of twenty-five percent five months later.

"With hindsight, I should have waited some more time to execute the first cut and then make the changes at one time. I would have minimized the trauma of cuts in several steps, as such trauma fundamentally shakes the morale of employees and the belief in the organization."

Takeaways

- Focus your change efforts on the low-hanging fruit, the ones that are easy to spot and fix, and gain credibility, supporters, and momentum.

- Ensure you have a committed change team and a solid sponsor before you proceed to make major change.

- Limit the number of change-team members. Chose the four or five who will bleed for you rather than the twenty who would take your side in a debate but change sides when things get rough.

- Choose your change team members according to the role each can play to complement the team, not according to their individual performance. It is like a football team: you don't want to have all your team members being excellent offense players without anybody minding your defense, do you?

In this chapter you learned that you need a good team, effective systems, and the right approach. We turn now to ideas and concepts about sustaining change for the long term.

10

Make change routine, not a strategic choice.

When change is one of the options, it naturally means there are alternatives.

Change is not an option; its a must for organizations that want to survive and prosper.

Change:
Make It Sustainable

Good job!

You have managed to change your organization.

It has been tough, tougher than anticipated, but it is finally done.

It took a bit longer than estimated but it is now changed.

Now, new questions come to your mind:

Will the change be sustainable for the long term?

Will things revert to the previous status if the drivers of change depart?

And what will happen if and when you leave? How much of everything you have changed will remain?

In this chapter, you will be exposed to concepts to help you make change sustainable—managing resistance, expanding the change agents deeper in your organization, increasing the commitment.

You will learn how to make the benefits of change visible and identify the people who will support you when difficulties start coming along.

Manage Resistance to Change and Achieve Longer-Term Sustainability

Have the change milestones been achieved easily?

Did you face resistance?

Do you still feel that some people are not convinced of the change even though it has been completed?

People will resist. The degree of resistance depends on how much they win or lose personally from the change. It also depends on the level of discomfort they are experiencing relative to their current situation, the status quo.

Managing resistance is a key component of implementing a successful change. You can manage resistance successfully if you can give the right answer to the seemingly simple question that exists in everybody's mind:

What is in it for me?

- You need to show to each function, department, and key person separately what he or she will gain from change. Prepare the mindset of teams and individuals to receive change.

- •Will change affect their paycheck now or in the future? Show it.

- Will it affect their career prospects? Show that, too.

- Will it affect the overall company positioning, future prospects, and thus people's security and future with the company? Demonstrate it.

"If I wanted something different, I would not be here now, would I?"

Fair point. Most people who feel comfortable with the status quo are not exactly looking for change. Quite the opposite: people are looking for comfort and zest.

Categorize the various stakeholders according to type and resistance to change, then prepare a plan for dealing with them:

- "I want to change, but on my terms." These people are not satisfied with their current status and want things to change, but only according to how they think things should be, and they are not usually willing to work for it!

  They will support you only in the beginning, because they see you as a chance, but they will soon realize that you are more serious and a bigger threat for them.

  People like that can be good as part of teams, but don't make them leaders, as they may change direction according to their own objectives.

- "I will go along with you, but don't expect great things from me." These are the people who smile and agree with whatever you offer only because they want to survive.

  They agree in a vague, not an action-oriented, manner. They are usually so weak that they will not help you in any step of the process but will remain negative to neutral throughout the change process. They are called "residents."

  Identify those people early and manage through them. Talk to them face-to-face, acknowledge that you recognize their style. Give them the short and direct advice to either get on with the change or prepare to be managed out of the organization.

- "I will tag along as long as you benefit my career, then I will leave you and support somebody else who can offer me more." They are willing to play along only because they see change as an opportunity for them to move up in their careers or gain other personal objectives. These are the dangerous ones. Be careful.

  Identify them early. Then use them for the short term or for individual projects if there is no other alternative, but also be prepared to manage them out of the organization. Always keep in mind that they will turn their back the moment they see power switching to other hands.

- "I am satisfied with the status quo but want to try new things." These are people you can count on. They act upon logic and conviction. They are trustworthy managers who see change as an evolutionary process, and they want to see the company develop.

  There aren't too many of them. If half of your direct reports are in this category, you are a lucky manager and on the right track.

  Base your plan upon them. Trust and empower them. Give them additional responsibility and accountability. Recognize and promote them. If you work well with these people, you will be able to counterbalance all the resistance generated by the others.

Increase Ownership and Build Commitment on the Changes through "Change Ambassadors"

Once you have established a good level of understanding and alignment with your direct reports, start thinking about broadening your change coalition to include other levels in the organization.

Develop more change ambassadors. Choose people who have already worked for you in the change process—the drivers, the leaders of initiatives, the people who are hungry to show what they can do, the ones who see you and what you represent as an opportunity.

Where do you find change ambassadors?
Go two or three layers deeper in your organization and identify as many change ambassadors as possible.

Don't go too far down the organization. It will take too much time and effort, and it will dilute your focus and impact. Let the change ambassadors affect lower levels in the organization; don't try to do everything yourself.

In departments where the boss is a resident, identify change ambassadors who can balance their leader's slower pace. Create flames of change below and around "residents" so that the momentum is comparable to the rest of the organization.

How do you assign them as change ambassadors?
Include them in the various task forces, change teams, or brainstorming groups. Assign them lead positions in projects.

Keep a personal eye on them, talking to them in one-to-one meetings about the progress of the project or initiative they are leading and then guiding them through.

Recognize them at every opportunity. Sponsor the projects they are leading. Support them when things go tough for them. Clear out bottlenecks for them.

Recognition will work well for the change ambassadors, but it will also make them stand up as examples to follow, hopefully creating a wave of imitators.

The Author's Case
The Author
Healthcare, Singapore

Choosing the right forum and the right approach to send a message about change can deepen the commitment of the change ambassadors and add charisma to your image.

About 100 of us were participating in the opening speech of the new Intercontinental president kickoff meeting in Singapore (Tony Hooper, President of U.S. Medicines for Bristol-Myers Squibb Company.)

One of his main messages was related to increasing efficiency by "taking work out."

To demonstrate the point, he took the monthly ten-page Significant Events Report and, in a sharp manner, tore it apart in front of everybody.

"I want you to be either in front of a customer or in front of a competitor and not in your offices telling me your story on a piece of paper. I want to see your progress through your numbers. I want to hear it from jealous competitors."

Do you want to make change visible? Be prepared to make some noise, to tear up some old habits, to start doing things significantly differently.

Make Change Visible and
Win Minds and Hearts

Some people will tear the walls apart or create glass offices to send a message of transparency and openness.

Others will send fliers about change electronically or on paper every week to all employees, announcing the progress of the change.

Whatever your methodology, make sure that your message is visible from the early stages and that it stays with people for some time.

Importance of Sponsors

For every change, small or big, short or long term, it is essential to have the right backup in terms of support and sponsorship.

What do sponsors do?

Sponsors support you during phases of the change when decisions are made at a higher level than yours, such as when a decision about funding one of your major projects is being made two levels above yours.

Sponsors can be important when one or more of your change initiatives do not go as planned, when resistance starts building, and when the results are not favorable. You need a strong presence, a loud and powerful voice, to confirm his/her belief in you and to give you additional time or resources to press on with change.

Where can you find sponsors?

Sponsors are executives higher up in the management layers. The best and obvious sponsor should be your boss, but that is not always easy.

The next best choice is your boss's boss!

Other key sponsors can be found among executives one or two levels above your boss at the corporate level.

Get your boss to be your change sponsor

Your boss will be open and supportive when change is company-wide, a corporate initiative, or a dictated change.

Your boss will support you when change is "needed" in his/her wider territory, not only in yours. Expect, however, that your boss may be considerably less supportive when you are initiating an elective change.

Not all bosses work that way. Sometimes you will be working for a boss who lives and dreams change.

Take the chance and do most of it in any situation, but especially when you are choosing to change. This is the chance to drive change deeper, wider, and into many areas of the organization.

Your boss may be open to your ideas and attracted by the anticipated benefits but not necessarily willing to fully back you when the going gets tough, when things get political, or when people start complaining.

How do you convince your boss or someone else to be a sponsor?

- Increase communication with your boss and encourage his or her involvement in your efforts at every step of the way.

- Emphasize the importance of your project to the company and to his/her department or function.
- Demonstrate the gains the change promises, but most importantly, stress the risks if the change does not take place.

  Remember: The most important decisions, both in business and in life, are taken based on the risks, not on the opportunities.

- Most importantly, emphasize what the prospective sponsor has to gain by supporting you. When appropriate, show others, especially those above him/her, how supportive and involved he is. Give him/her part of the credit and recognition.

Sounding Board

Do you at times feel uncertain about a strategy you are taking?

Are there times when you need to bounce ideas off someone?

Are there things that you do not always feel comfortable sharing with your boss?

The sounding board helps you see things more clearly, provides an unbiased second opinion, and builds your confidence about an issue or a decision.

The sounding board is an informal forum where trusted individuals give you advice without seeking a personal benefit and without expecting that you will do as they recommend.

Listen to each of them, but always make your own decision as you move forward.

Profile of a sounding board

- A sounding board can have a single member or go up to six or seven people. The number depends on how openly you accept the ideas and comments of others, the complexity of the issues on hand, as well as the availability of credible sounding-board members.

- Members need to know you well, your style, what you aim to accomplish, and the situation and issues.

- Choose people who understand the issue and will give you feedback directly, without needing lengthy discussions.

- You can choose from your colleagues or those from elsewhere in your company at the same level as you, above you, or even below you, as well as managers with whom you worked in the past, family members, or friends.

- You can even choose your spouse. He/she knows you very well, regardless of his/her low expertise in the functional part of your job or the complexity of the issue. She or he can give you good support and sound advice through her or his own perspective, usually softening things and calming reactions down, helping you arrive at a more mature decision.

Maximize the effectiveness of your sounding board

- Keep the members of your sounding-board updated about the progress of those changes you are implementing so they can stay aware of the developments and be able to jump with suggestions quickly.

- Categorize your sounding-board members according to their area of expertise. One person might be more suitable to advise you about re-engineering issues. Another might be better qualified to talk about people-related matters.

- Choose when to seek advice from sounding board members. When you believe you are going too fast on a project and you sense that you need to talk to a calmer voice, you need to identify which sounding board member can do this. It might be someone who can slow you down or someone who can give you speed.

- Do not call on your sounding-board only when you need them. Keep the relationship healthy by being there for them when they need you.

- Always thank your mentors and show appreciation of their support.

What if you cannot have a sounding board?

Story has it that Aristotle Onassis, the Greek tycoon, had a full-time lawyer whose only job was to debate him on all the major issues so that Onassis would be convinced that he challenged each issue enough.

Since most people around him would not easily go against his will, another benefit for Onassis was that at least one person would have the courage to say "I disagree." (At that time and culture, courage was indeed needed to say no to a person of Onassis' stature).

You can do the same, or almost the same, thing. Engage a lawyer or a consultant on a part time basis. Or look around your floor and find a colleague who can play this role. Start with the easy issues and see how it goes.

If everything else fails, walk on the beach and talk to yourself! Sounds crazy? Ask Louis Gerstner, the successful ex-President of IBM, who used to walk on the beach in Florida and talk to himself, usually finding solutions for many of his issues.

The difference between a sounding board and a mentor

Let's keep the two separate. The mentor assists you with your personal development and your career issues. It's a big brother or sister or a friend who knows you better than most people and who always wants what is best for you. Mentoring is an ongoing process about the same main subject—you!

A sounding-board member is concerned with strategy and operations. This person needs to respond quickly and to the point on a very specific issue.

The Cassandras*

Is all the advice you receive from people around you well intended?

Should you listen to Cassandras whose objectives are malintended?

Do not dismiss the Cassandras of the world. These people whisper in your ears about the risks, what goes on behind your back, gossip, etc. Listen to them and discount their words as you deem appropriate, but do listen! Sometimes, they give you very useful information that allows you to re-align before issues get bigger and more difficult to manage.

---

* In mythology, Cassandra was the daughter of Priam, the King of Troy. She had guessed that the wooden horse the Greeks gave the Trojans as gift was a bad ornament and begged her father not to take it into the city. You know the rest.

Takeaways

- Each participant in a change expects to gain something from participating. Identify what these "somethings" are and give them to the participants.

- Describe the end result of change, package it well, and communicate it to your organization. People will commit earlier and more fully if they know what they are working toward.

- You need the sponsors most when things start going badly and everybody else is jumping ship. Then you need this voice from higher up to support you in keeping things rolling.

- If you can't find a sounding board, buy one. Hire a lawyer or a change expert and ask them to criticize your plans.

In the preceding three chapters, you learned how to evolve an organization through understanding, implementing, and sustaining change.

In the next chapter, you will discover five practical and easy-to-implement systems for managing performance.

11

Systems rationalize options and take biases and old beliefs out.

Five Systems to
Manage Performance

Is it difficult to manage performance in your company? Do you know the right parameters to manage performance? Do you find it increasingly challenging to monitor it?

Performance is one of the most critical and, at the same time, one of the toughest areas to manage for companies. You need to identify the most important areas, then you need to set systems in place to measure each area.

In this chapter you will see the five most important performance metrics and you will learn how to:

- Be ready to act before your competitors, with the right level of competitive pressure by identifying the future sales trends and assumptions.

- Maximize internal company efficiencies by setting up a well-integrated mechanism to manage product flow.

- Improve the company's financial performance by tightly managing cash flow.

- Stay on top of your competitive game by beating your internal and external competitors through benchmarking.

- Create a growing and sustainable, year-after-year return on investment through managing your company's business leverage.

Here are five specific systems to manage performance successfully:

Manage your Top Line and
Drive Top Performance

Does your company grow when the market grows? What do you do to stay above the water, to perform better than the rest of your competitors, when the market declines?

To manage your top line is to anticipate the industry trends, to identify their impact on your business planning, and eventually to translate these trends in terms of their impact on your products' market share.

To manage investment plans, most companies use a strategic plan (usually a 3–6 year plan) for long-term business planning, a business plan to manage current financial performance, and quarterly or monthly reviews to manage the shorter term.

A few companies, however, have distinct systems to manage sales.

"The Rolling Forecast System": A sales-forecasting and business-planning tool for maximizing resource allocation and focus

Jim's Case
Jim Atkinson, Director of Beckman Coulter Intl SA
Healthcare, Nyon, Switzerland

Jim says: "The ability to forecast is heavily dependent on setting in place the right systems which, with the right leadership, can lead to superior performance.

"As the leader of a distributor organization with over 70 dealers, we were always being urged to improve our forecasting. As a matter of fact, I was told that it was impossible to accurately forecast product sales even for the current month.

"I set about constructing a twice-monthly, simplified process of review with the order processing, logistics, and finance teams that involved two meetings of no more than an hour to validate the area managers' monthly forecasts and highlight any blockages, shortfalls, or over-performance. In the first meeting, people wanted to talk in detail about every order, but I insisted on an overview approach that established whether the substantial orders would be shipped by the end of the month, and after a few months we were becoming very accurate.

"I had to personally get involved and set up the process so that everyone understood the aim and stayed focused. Now, I don't even need to attend, as we always know where we'll end up for the month without surprises."

The Rolling Forecast System enables you to form a base to link the short-, mid-, and long-term plans for the top line. It is a spreadsheet-based method that provides you with accurate forecasts, combining historic data with updated rolling forecasts for the next 12 to 24 months.

This is how the Rolling Forecast System works:

- It is based on historic data (2–3 years back) along with the monthly forecasting statistics. The forecasting statistics are important since they show your forecasting accuracy and trend. This filters out the biases that might exist from over-optimism or over-conservatism in forecasting by the key stakeholders, such as the sales and marketing executives.

- The sales and marketing departments prepare their own forecasts based on the assumptions in the marketing plan as well as on the latest market information and trends. Each department prepares its plans separately, then they meet to have an assumptions-based discussion for each product. The aim is to convince management of their forecasting assumptions. This healthy debate leads to well-balanced, challenged, and more-accurate sales forecasts.

- The difference between what you plan and what you deliver is the "forecasting variance." The level of forecasting variance allowed—the differences between what s forecasted and what actually happens—depends on the time horizon you are forecasting for. The smaller the period, the smaller the percent variance allowed: around 10% for next month, within 10–20 percent for the following three months, and up to 30% for the following 8 to 12 months. The bigger the size of the sales of a product, the greater the need for more efficient forecasting. For example, a variance of one percent on $100 million sales is more important than ten percent on $1 million sales. Thus it is logical to expect that the smaller the size of a brand, the higher the expected percentage variations that can take place.

What do we do with these revised forecasts?

These new forecasts become your new targets, your new projection of revised sales. Focus your organization towards updated and realistically stretched targets on a continuous, rolling, basis.

Another use of the updated forecast is in the supply chain, which can adjust their manufacturing and supply-chain resources management to your new assumptions, thereby creating additional efficiencies.

- The Sales Rolling Forecast sheet is automatically linked to another spreadsheet that consolidates the data for each product toward the total for your product group/category. This, in turn, automatically links to the total company spreadsheet. Every time you change one cell, all spreadsheets should automatically change.

A good information-systems team should be able to create this spreadsheet-based system, adopted for your company's brands and processes, within a week or two.

A more-detailed description of the system and a sample of a product is on the facing page.

THE SALES ROLLING FORECAST SYSTEM

Budget

	1st Quarter 2006	2nd Quarter 2006	3rd Quarter 2006	4th Quarter 2006	Full Year 2006	Change vs Budget
	Forecast	Forecast	Forecast	Forecast		
Product X	100	100	101	102	403	
Product Y	60	60	60	60	240	
Product Z	20	25	30	33	108	
Total	180	185	191	195	751	

Original sales targets set for the year as Budgeted forecasts for each key product.

Projection1

	1st Quarter 2006	2nd Quarter 2006	3rd Quarter 2006	4th Quarter 2006	Full Year 2006	Change vs Budget
	Actual	Forecast	Forecast	Forecast		
Product X	95	103	99	100	397	-1%
Product Y	55	57	58	59	229	-5%
Product Z	22	28	33	36	119	10%
Total	172	188	190	195	745	-1%
vs budget	96%	102%	99%	100%		

1 quarter into the year, actual results are updated for 1st quarter. Achievement vs budget tracked.

Forecasts for the coming quarters also updated. Variance between new set of forecasts tracked vs previous set of forecasts (budget).

Projection2

	1st Quarter 2006	2nd Quarter 2006	3rd Quarter 2006	4th Quarter 2006	Full Year 2006	Change vs Budget
	Actual	Actual	Forecast	Forecast		
Product X	95	103	99	98	395	-2%
Product Y	55	57	58	61	231	-4%
Product Z	22	30	33	35	120	11%
Total	172	190	190	194	746	-1%
vs budget	96%	103%	99%	99%		
vs projection 1	100%	101%	100%	99%		

Update process repeated regularly, revising actuals and consequently forecasts. Achievement tracked vs each set of previous forecasts, to have a systematic sense of trends in forecasting accuracy.

Maximize Efficiencies by Tightly Managing the Product Flow

Have you been in situations where you lost sales because you faced out-of-stock situations as the supply-chain plan could not keep up with the changing demand? Have you faced situations where you were left with millions of dollars of inventory in the warehouse, idle and costing you money because the forecast was over-optimistic?

Good inventory management will improve your cash flow as well as save money so that you can devote those resources to more productive activities in other parts of your organization.

Good inventory management will also limit your exposure in case of volatilities, such as abrupt foreign-exchange variations.

Giovanni's Case
Giovanni Tardelli, South Europe VP
Logistics/Distribution, Milan, Italy

Giovanni demonstrates that, in addition to having the right systems, the company needs to have the right mindset.

He says: "The director of Technical Operations in a Southern-European subsidiary was starting his presentation as part of my orientation, having just come in as the new Regional VP. He proudly showed me his first slide with his department's objective/mission: 'Never let the business be out of stock of any product.' He stood up, looked around to his smiling team members, and stated that they had never faced an out-of-stock situation during the past two years.

"Now, why wasn't I happy about that? Why wasn't I impressed? Quite the contrary, I would say... I felt low efficiency, high level of comfort, and not enough stretch..."

What do we consider good inventory management?

How can we define what the optimum level of inventory is?

This is when the "Inventory Management System" comes into place and helps you in three different ways.

First, good inventory management of a single product minimizes the time a product spends in each inventory activity while it is in your hands (from the ordering of raw material, manufacturing, and inventory on hand) so that the product is as close as possible to being "just in time" at each step.

Second, it allows you to balance all manufacturing and supply-chain items in a manner that enables you to avoid excess capacity.

Third, it helps you determine the optimum levels of inventory, either by doing a superb job in managing the process or through the simple method of lowering the inventory level of one or two products far enough to create out of stock situations. Then you know your limits and you keep your inventories at a slightly higher level than the minimum you just discovered.

Sometimes, you need take a step of a cliff just so you can feel the blood in your veins running.

Once you achieve the optimum level of inventory at each link in the supply chain, then you move on to additional improvements, using the Inventory Management System:

- Categorize the products according to their level of sensitivity or difficulty in managing their inventory and assign an additional inventory as "fat" on top of the "optimum stock level" that you had identified earlier:

  A: Products that you cannot afford to run out of stock on (i.e., products with long manufacturing lead times).

  B: Products that have constraints or issues in manufacturing (i.e., technically challenging products requiring infrequent, specially controlled manufacturing runs).

  C: Products that have high growth patterns (i.e., recently launched, seasonal products).

THE INVENTORY MANAGEMENT SYSTEM

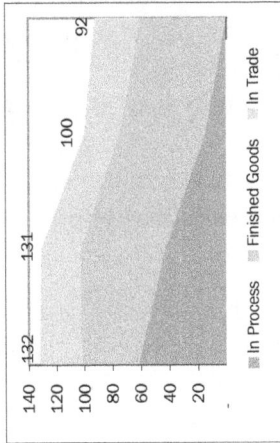

Visual presentation of stock levels distinguishing between layers: process, finished goods and in-trade.

Total stock level broken down into different layers represented in days on hand at different layers.

Actual & estimated stock levels tracked vs targets identifying the variances.

Qualitative section providing rationale on variances.

	1st Quarter 2006 Actual	2nd Quarter 2006 Actual	3rd Quarter 2006 Forecast	4th Quarter 2006 Forecast
In Process	62	43	15	-
Finished Goods	40	60	60	60
In Trade	30	28	25	32
Product Z	**132**	**131**	**100**	**92**
Target	**95**	**95**	**95**	**95**
Gap	-37	-36	-5	3

Comments

Product Z started the yr with buildup from past yr due to supply issues foreseen in the second half of 2006

D: All others. That level of inventory was set for each product and that was your targeted level of inventory.

- Challenge the factory and re-establish manufacturing orders and frequency of production so that the inventory level on hand remains at low levels.

- Limit further the stocks at your primary customers, thus tightening the inventory amount out of your control.

- Have a progressive mechanism in place as a common communication and management tool, such as the "Inventory Management Map."

"Cash is King": A System to Manage Your Cash Flow

"Cash is King!" shouts Dominique Jacquets, professor of finance at INSEAD, one of the best business schools globally. True! Very true!

The primary reason why companies go bankrupt or are bought at a bargain price by a rival company is poorly managing cash flow. More than any other reason, including lack of sales or making the wrong investment choices, cash flow makes or breaks companies.

The process below will help you identify and focus on the key cash-flow management areas and help you give your company a healthy longevity:

- Account Receivables: Prioritize customers according to ability to pay (nothing new there!), but put strict criteria on your larger customers. This may sound contradictory. Bigger customers pay sooner and with guarantees (when appropriate), but we also provide higher discounts to them. Smaller customers gain on cost of money by paying later, but with a much smaller discount margin.

- Managing Discounts: Discounts to customers rarely provide sustainable long-term value. Rather, they are short-term competitive tools that lead to waste of money and resources. It is the ultimate demand for your product (the demand by the actual users of your product) that builds the brand equity that determines your competitive level, not your discounts. Discounts simply provide short-term sales results, increasing your inventory levels but affecting very little in terms of long-term, sustained purchases or usages.

I advise you to gradually stop giving discounts. Use them only when they are appropriate for well-defined, short-term cost/ benefit relationships, such as a product launch, to gain distribution or shelf access.

There are exceptions. Well-planned, short-term discounts can offer value as a complementary part of your plans. A quantity discount concept of, say, "buy 3 get 1 free," can encourage distribution to buy products in adequate quantities to satisfy seasonal or other demands (for example, the launch of new product) without compromising the list price of the product that distributors will later buy at the initial price.

- Managing Bad Debt: Bad debt is closely associated with the management of receivables. The overall survival of your company is at stake, so you have to be tough. If you believe in your product or service, then demand respect from your buyers and distributors. They show minimum respect by paying you on time, so demand this respect by being tough in your collections. Don't be afraid to take to court customers who don't pay. Do this well before the amounts become unrecoverable.

  Do you lose customers by having such a tough policy? Well, of course you do. But you lose fewer if you communicate your policy to each customer at the beginning of your relationship, and if you have alternatives, you will not lose sales of your product to your final users.

  By the way, the same goes for governments that fail to meet their obligations. I don't know of many companies that have chosen the court route against the government and did not come away with their money.

Even though you expose yourself to possible retaliation, you should not rule out court action as the last resort.

Involving industry associations where the problem of collections or non-payment is across companies is also a useful strategy.

Most importantly, prepare yourself, your organization, and especially your management for losing some potential sales by applying strict cash-flow management policies.

To succeed in this game, you need to know when to say "no" and when to stop selling.

Stay on Top of The Competitive Game through Benchmarking

How do you know if you perform well? How better or worse are you doing versus your key competitors in the market place? What do you need to do to beat them and do so consistently?

Benchmarking is a key system that companies use to measure and manage performance.

In most cases, benchmarking focuses on internal targets. Targets are usually set by headquarters, based on previous history and future performance expectations. We all have a set of numbers to meet, the so-called "budget" for each financial year or so. These are the internal sales and/or profit targets each business unit is asked to achieve.

Such methodology is archaic, limiting and distracting from the focus from the real battlefield: the market place.

Traditional budget-related targets (e.g., sales and profits) are the result of negotiations between you, your organization, and your management; they do not fully reflect market reality.

The budget-related targets that most companies use are simply the minimum targets they have to achieve, the minimum performance the company expects and a way to award incentives at the end of the year. Nothing more than that.

Successful companies complement such internal, budget-related targets with external, market-share-related objectives.

These companies also have incentive systems built around those internal and external targets.

1) External benchmarking through market share

This is the ultimate performance measurement.

The environment, as in competitors and market trends, should be taken into account.

Estimate the market trends in terms of growth or decline, assume competitors' movements (entries, re-launches, commercial activities, etc), and then map out your own market-share expectations.

"A company without a market-share target is a company without a strategy."

2) Intracompany, regional benchmarking

We have all participated in company-wide presentations where the performance of the various business units is compared. We have all felt proud when our results were better than those of other units and, let's admit, we have felt uncomfortable when our results were below those of others.

Internal benchmarking is an extremely useful tool for setting performance targets and basing organizational targets on what other countries or business units do.

Effective benchmarking could include:

●●Internal budget related targets (i.e., percentage growth versus targets or previous years).

● Market-share achievement on key products.

● Talent developed and exported to higher positions in the organization.

● Responses to the various company initiatives (e.g., marketing development, inventory management).

Internal benchmarking determines whether you are going to get a promotion in the organization. This is what management sees on a daily basis and this is how your image will be built or weakened.

Manage Leverage and Maximize Performance

Leverage is the variance between your incremental investment in relation to the incremental return.

For example, if you grow your sales by 10% and your profit by 15%, you have created a positive leverage of 5%, thus increasing performance by using less investment or by utilizing the same level of investment more productively.

Why is leverage so important? According to many general managers, it is the most important word in any business dictionary. It reflects the resource allocation you are making across resources and products and your success in increasing the return on investment.

Leverage is widely used in all new investment evaluations as well as in comparisons of product groups within a business unit or area of responsibility.

Takeaways

- Sales forecasting helps you beat the industry trends and all your competitors with it.

- Tight inventory management frees up resources so you can use them in the competitive field.

- Managing bad debt is not only about money; it is foremost about respect. Demand minimum respect for your products or services by getting your money on time.

- Well-set and well-monitored benchmarking not only improves the performance of your business unit, but it can move you to higher positions as well.

- A successful manager identifies the expected business leverage that the company expects and perform higher.

You have now learned five practical systems to manage the key elements of your Profit & Loss Statement. In the next chapter, you will discover how to achieve a fast-moving and disciplined organizational pace and then to sustain it at optimum performance levels.

12

For prioritization to be optimal, it needs to be discriminatory toward the biggest opportunities. The higher the level of discrimination, the higher the probability of success.

Manage Organizational Pace

Are all the functions of your unit moving at different speeds? Are some projects lagging behind while others are ahead of schedule? Does this misalignment make it difficult to move the company forward in a well-coordinated manner?

Managing organizational pace is at the heart of the systems-management approach. It seeks the right balance, the correct heartbeat, that each organization needs. It blends together strategies on the one hand and people and behavior on the other into a dynamic combination.

How do you create the right balance, the optimum organizational pace?

Find the balance of prioritization, discipline, and speed that al- lows your organization to meet and exceed targets.

You have to get the right balance; but always remember, we are talking about a *balance*.

Optimize Priorities and Maximize
Resource-Allocation and Focus

Why is it difficult to prioritize?

First you have to make the *right* choices. This is not always easy. Stephan Thiroloix, Vice President/General Manager for Bristol-Myers Squibb Company in France, says choice is not about what you do but about what you currently don't do.

Prioritizing is difficult because priorities are set by various stakeholders who are not necessarily aligned with each other.

Most priorities are set by management, either through setting objectives (i.e. budgeting) or changing strategies. You also set priorities as the leader of the company or unit. These reflect the specific issues and opportunities you are facing.

Finally, priorities are sometimes set by the environment, government, or competition. Changes in priorities can result in new policies, new pricing pressures, and new trade union issues.

Optimizing priorities assumes that you de-prioritize and drop projects. It is like a juggling act with many balls. You must choose which balls to drop and drop them fast!

By proactively choosing which ones to drop and dropping them sooner, you keep the focus on the more important ones. Otherwise, you may drop some big ones as well. The more projects you drop, the more focused and aligned your company will be.

For prioritization to be optimal, you need to discriminate in favor of the biggest opportunities. The higher the level of discrimination, the more suitable the level of prioritization.

George's Case
George Havic, Regional General Manager
Investment Banking, Zurich, Switzerland

George will tell you that discriminatory and blunt prioritization work better than long hours of work and anxiety to do everything right.

"Following a two-day intensive review meeting with my regional boss, Franco Taviari, we were at the airport waiting for his delayed-by-two-hours flight to London.

"I was passionately working through my mobile phone trying to catch up on many pending issues, much to the surprise of Franco who said: 'You are always working—during the coffee breaks, while in the car, during the weekends, now at the airport on a Friday night following two days of successful reviews. Why? Why do you do this to yourself?'

"'Well,' I replied, 'I am busy, that's why. I have gotten the new job as regional head for Central Europe and I want to do well quickly!'

"'OK,' he said, 'I understand this, but you are not going to do it by working more hours. You were already working too much. You need to prioritize more effectively. For example,' he said, 'I overheard you talking to someone in Malta. What was that about?'

"'Malta is new in my territory, and although the opportunity is very small, we are trying to boost the business there. The partner we have there is eager and demanding....'

"'How much does Malta represent in your total regional sales? One percent? Two?' Franco asked.

"'It's not much in terms of size, but the partner is good and I don't want to let him down,' I replied.

"'Forget Malta' said Franco emphatically, with a tone of voice that did not leave much to challenge. 'Take it out of your list of projects, your targets, the whole thing.'

"'What do you mean? How...'

"Franco continued, 'How? I'll tell you how. Call our partner there and tell him that you will not call him again because you have prioritized him in the lower end of your list. I want you to focus on the biggest markets first. When you fully maximize the biggest opportunities, then you could possibly talk about Malta. This is how I want you to treat this market.'

"I did not exactly forget about Malta but I have definitely taken it out of my list of priorities.

"Franco's lesson was a long-standing and impactful one for all the 'Maltas' that were taking time and focus away from me."

"Top Five Priorities"

This is a simple and effective method in managing priorities for the short term, a period of two to three months.

The "Top Five Priorities" is a list of critical projects that will affect your performance during the defined period and the achievement of which will impact your whole organization.

This is how you build a successful Top Five Priorities system:

- Identify and list your Top Five Priorities for the next two month period. These are the projects whose contribution to your targets for the next one to three months will be critical.

- The list should include projects or activities that will command focus and effort and determine your success or failure for this period. These priorities should not include routine projects or projects with general descriptions.

- Renew the Top Five Priorities every month for the next three months.

- "Cascade" your Top Five Priorities down your organization in a tree-like approach.

- First do yours and share them with your direct reports. Have your direct reports prepare their own, aligned with yours. Then they do the same with their subordinates, and so on down the line.

You'll know when you have a well-aligned and coordinated team when you call one of your direct reports and simply ask "what is going on?" and they instinctively start going over their Top Five Priorities, one by one!

Walter's Case
Walter Billington, Business Unit Head
Fast-Moving Consumer Goods, UK

Walter, a strong systems believer, advises not to get discouraged when people don't always align. He has a good example to convince us of that.

Company or Business Unit Name

TOP 5 PRIORITIES - Jan/Feb/March 2007

	Work Priorities	In Charge	Deadline/Reviews
1	**Strategic Planning** - Initial assumption-setting from the brands - Contingency plans prepared	**John Smith (GM)** Team: Brand Managers Team: Finance Director	Feb 15
2	**New Product Launches** - TV Campaign rollout - Distribution coverage of 75% achieved	**Wendy Jones (Marketing Dir)** Lynn White (Brand Mgr) Jonathan Spike (Sales Dir)	March 30
3	**Salary Increases** - Review of proposals by function - Discussion with unions to be initiated - Final plans in place	**Tom McGrath (HR Dir)** Team: Function Heads Team: Tom McGrath	Jan 20 Feb 1 March 30
4	**Manufacturing Site Transfer of Product Alpha** - Action plan to be presented for approval to the operating committee - Plan initiation	**Michel Gonzalez (Factory Dir)**	Jan 15 Feb 15
5	**New Year's Employee Celebration** - Event agenda finalization - Vendors selection completed - Event	**Tom McGrath (HR Dir)**	Jan 10 Jan 15 Feb 15

"I had a really tough time convincing one of my direct reports, a business unit head, to effectively use the Top Five Priorities. He would prepare his own and report it to me (simply because it was my request), but he would not reinforce it to his direct reports or show any appreciation of this system.

"After a couple of years, he decided to move to a small, local company as their general manager.

"When I jokingly told him that he would finally forget about the systems, Top Five and the rest, he turned to me and, with all seriousness, said, 'Your systems are the first things I will implement when I go to the new job. As a matter of fact, I will start with the Top Five Priorities.'

"It seemed very strange to me, so I asked him what had changed over the last two years, since I had not been able to convince him about the usefulness of systems.

"He looked straight into my eyes and said, 'The difference is that now I will be the boss and need to align everybody else around me.'"

Attain a High Level of Discipline
and Maximize Speed and Alignment

Manage both discipline and the speed and alignment of the various functions in your organization and across the people who work for you.

Discipline is the one of the most important and underrated elements of successful management. By managing discipline, you manage organizational pace.

Discipline brings together two very important things: what the mind creates (targets, strategies, processes) and what the heart wants (motivation, trust, mental capacity).

The better the balance and blend of the two, the more successful and long-lived your career will be.

How do you manage discipline?

You master the art of discipline management by managing empowerment, by balancing priorities and functions, and by distinguishing between the tasks that need to be done and the people who are expected to do them.

Empowerment

"When we have good leaders, we should empower them and then leave them alone." This is what traditional management theory states.

If you still believe that, then read on and be ready to change your mind!

Empowering good leaders and leaving them alone can result in people, even gifted people, creating their own pace that is not necessarily aligned with the rest of the organization.

Excessive and unbounded empowerment of single individuals can lead to arrogance among these people and lead other employees to sense that you have created a system of favoritism.

Empowerment without systems can produce chaotic or even rigid styles, depending on the personalities of the managers who are in control.

Don't misunderstand the message. Empowerment is dynamic, but not all empowerment is, nor is it dynamic under all conditions.

Yes, empowered people can appreciate the trust and the room to produce, but good people can also maximize their potential and productivity within a more systematic framework.

Here is the proposal

The more empowerment you give, the more systems you should have in place to manage it.

Empowered individuals can maximize their productivity in an environment with clearly-defined and controlled boundaries.

As you see on the graph (next page), the better-defined the action framework, the more productive the individual can become.

Find the right balance among (a) the level of talent, (b) the control level required, and (c) the empowerment level. The higher

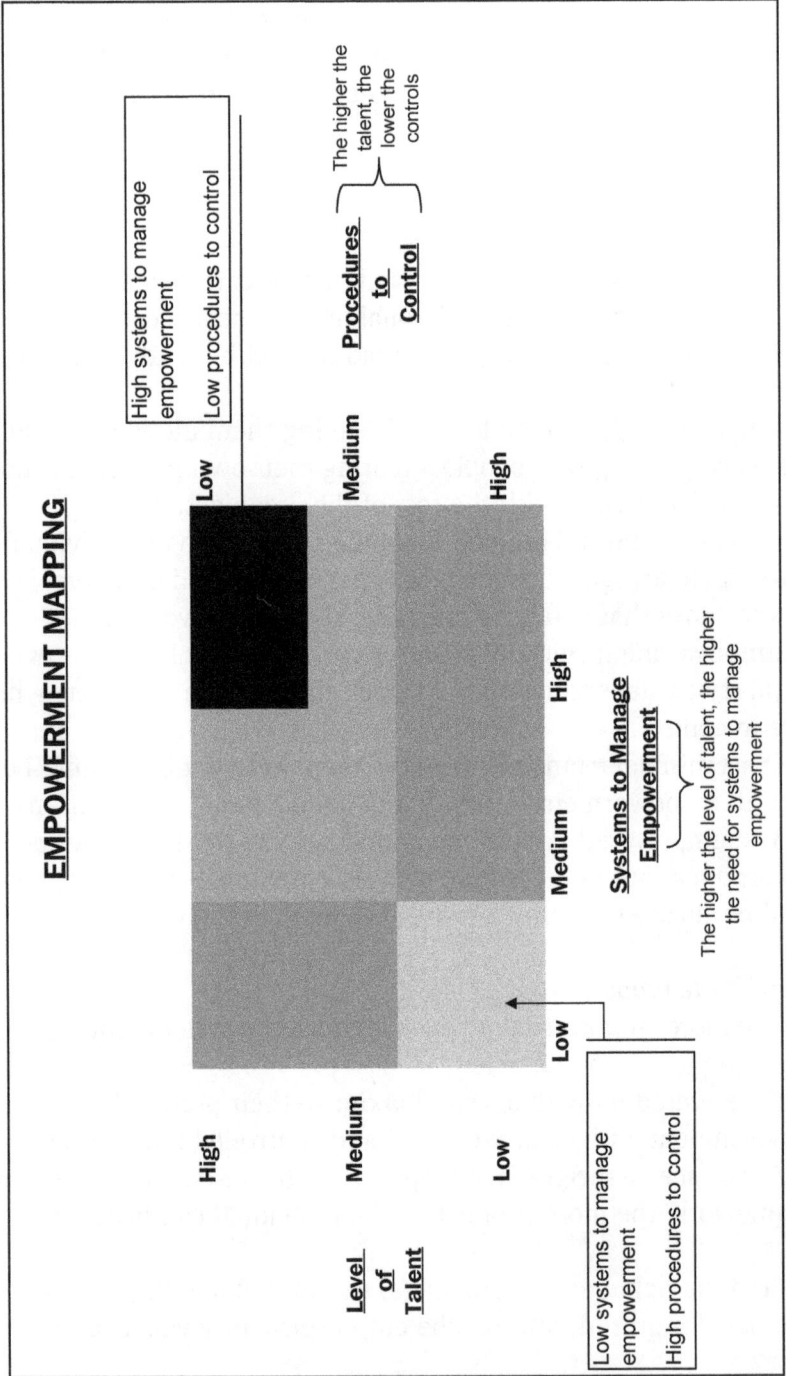

EMPOWERMENT MAPPING

High systems to manage empowerment

Low procedures to control

The higher the talent, the lower the controls

Procedures
to
Control

Level
of
Talent

High

Medium

Low

Low

Medium

High

Systems to Manage Empowerment

The higher the level of talent, the higher the need for systems to manage empowerment

Low systems to manage empowerment

High procedures to control

the talent level, the lower the level of control and the higher the level of empowerment should be. The opposite is equally true. Once you find this balance and define the boundaries, only then can you let people run their own shows. Then keep with this systematic approach.

"Pressure Mapping": A Pace-Management Tool for Balancing Pressure across Departments and Projects

Are functions and people performing at different levels? Do some need to move faster or more efficiently?

Do you sense that some departments are more pressured than others?

Pressure mapping is a useful tool for balancing the pressure across your organization and managing the organizational pace. It is based on, and is an extension of, The Strategy Brain Workshop concept presented in an earlier chapter.

This is how it works:

- Start with your project listing from The Strategy Brain Workshop.

- Break the projects down as they apply to each department or function in your organization and add any additional projects or important routine tasks (such as budget preparation, monthly financial reporting, etc.).

- Map out all projects throughout the year. You will easily spot where the pressure points are. You may notice that a specific function is heavily loaded compared to the others.

For example, suppose you notice that several projects are planned to take place at the same time across functions. Adjust the stress by postponing one or more projects to a later time.

COMPANY OR BUSINESS UNIT NAME

2007 EFFICIENCY & PRESSURE MAPPING

INITIATIVES	LEVEL OF IMPORTANCE	RESPONSIBLE	1Q07	2Q07	3Q07	4Q07
Across Company (involving more than 1 dept)						
- Strategic Session, "The Strategist"	XX	N Portier				
- Benchmarking System Application	XX	E Trenton				
- Business Dev't Project	XXXX	J Hedan				
		E Morales				
DEPARTMENT: Marketing						
- Product X Launch	XXXX	J Lohre				
- Geographic Expansion of Product Y	XX	J Vasquez				
- Marketing Training	X	A Morales				
- Pilot Testing in Product Z	XXX	J Curtis				
DEPARTMENT: Human Resources						
- Reward & Recognition System	XXX	A Abdalla				
- Recruitment Efficiency Plan	XXXX	D Barnes				
- Employee Survey	XX	W Billington				
DEPARTMENT: Sales						
- Category Management Rollout	X	V Petrovic				
- Sales Training Program	XXXX	D Wilson				
- New Account Plans	XX	G Tardelli				

Ranking Notes
1) XXXXX: Highest Priority
2) Pressure Level

Legend:
- Very High
- High
- Average
- Below Average

How do you adjust the pressure?

You adjust pressure by:

- Postponing some of the projects to a later date.

- Reducing the involvement of the specific function in some of those cross-company projects so it can focus on its own unit and function.

- Adding resources to a department or project for a period of time, enough to get through the stretch without compromising productivity or speed.

Don't waste energy on the wrong things. The passion and pressure you put into a project should be proportionate to the return you expect from this specific project and should be adjusted according to the probability of success.

Takeaways

- Optimum prioritization assumes that you de-prioritize and drop projects. The more projects you drop, the more focused and aligned your company will be.

- Avoid the allure of empowerment by managing the paradox: The more you want to empower, the more well-defined and controlled the boundaries of empowerment should be.

- Pressure that is well balanced and equally allocated across functions and projects increases value much more than the value of its contributing parts.

Now that you know how to achieve the right organizational pace through balancing strategies and people, you are ready to deep-dive into time management.

13

Management is a juggling act with many balls. You are trying to balance too many things and you know some of them will drop. Choosing which balls to keep is important.

More important, however, is to know which balls to drop, and to drop them fast.

Manage Your Time Effectively and Gain Focus Where It Really Counts!

Do unplanned things get in the way and keep you from finishing tasks on time? Does your phone ring all the time both on and off work, taking valuable time away from your work and personal time? Do your family, your spouse, or your children complain that you don't have enough time for them because you are always working?

General managers, like all responsible and busy executives, work long hours. It is quite common that a "normal" day lasts ten to twelve hours, not just the eight-hour working day that employees enjoy.

Good time management is a key element of success for a general manager.

First, it increases your ability to allocate your time to important issues. Efficient priorities are based on the impact of each activity on the business, the importance of the issue within the hierarchy, and the urgency under which the discussion or decision takes place.

Second, it increases the quality and speed of decision making. Good time management devotes an optimum amount of time to each issue. More time is given to important issues, while less critical issues are given either less time or no time at all; they are postponed or delegated to lower layers in the organization.

Finally, good time management allows you to be available—available to employees for leading, motivating, encouraging, and guiding, and available to your loved ones with enough uninterrupted quality time.

In this chapter, you will see simple and efficient ways to master your time management at the same time as you learn methods for balancing your time between leading, strategizing, and executing.

You will also learn simple and proven methods for managing routine things like daily agendas, meetings, and one-to-one discussions.

Daily Time-Management Formula

Wouldn't it be nice to have a golden formula to manage time?

Well, there is such a formula! Although it might seem overly simplistic, you can define management productivity as:

Importance of Activity x Hours Worked x Intensity

Choose the most important projects or activities and focus on them. When you devote your time to the activities with the highest impact on your business, you will immediately increase your personal effectiveness in the business. At the same time, you will get rid of all the routine, low-level, and marginal activities.

Although it is understandable that a person's capacity to produce falls as the number of hours at work increases beyond 8 or 9, one can also be open to accept that a person who works longer hours will produce more work. For example, between two people of same abilities and responsibilities, it is logical to assume that the person who works more hours will have a higher output. It might seem overly simplistic, but it is true.

Some people believe that working a small number of hours but working efficiently is enough. That would be true only in the case that a person's performance is being evaluated in isolation but not when it is seen within the broader competitive environment such as the other general managers.

Raise your intensity on each project according to its importance and the effect of the activity on your performance. Manage the pressure by adjusting the sense of urgency, the frequency, and intensity of your follow-ups.

Do you have many important projects at the same time? If so, increase the hours worked to manage them through and increase the intensity of your efforts.

Do you have a small number of high-impact projects requiring high intensity? In this case, limit the number of projects you are dealing with, and heighten the intensity you bring to them.

Do you find yourself working more than eight or nine hours every day? No decent leader works beyond the normal eight or nine hours per day for the company. Absolutely not. While leaders may continue to work beyond normal working hours for "company matters," their motive should be different. It should be personal. Leaders work more because they want to be better, advance their careers, improve their pending performance or salary reviews, or beat the internal competitors.

The company should be able to appreciate this behavior and the benefits it receives accordingly.

When are you going beyond "normal" working hours for a general manager? You become a workaholic when your find yourself working long hours simply because you cannot catch up with things, because you feel insecure, or because you believe that only by working long hours will you do your best.

You cannot sustain working like that. Sooner or later, your performance will reflect, not the hours you have put in, but the frustration and fatigue that come from those long hours. Your family will be affected the most as your time for them becomes less and less.

Eventually, that situation will lead to your derailment.

If you find yourself doing this, take a break. A long break. Talk to your family and friends, your mentors, your boss. Identify the root cause and deal with it.

Strategic Time-Management System

Is it challenging to jump from a simple project follow-up one minute to a strategic session the next and to a hiring interview the minute after that?

How do you adjust your style, speed, and attention as you move from activity to activity?

Dan Domenech, Senior Human Resources Director for Bristol-Myers Squibb Company, advises general managers, as he has advised me, to allocate their time effectively through the use of a strategic time-management system. He gives some good hints on how that interchange, that blend, can take place effectively.

The graph on the next page demonstrates that, as one's career evolves, there is a parallel evolution in the mix of basic characteristics towards excellence on the job. This same graph applies to you as general manager.

Let's look at how you can manage each component separately and then how you can make the perfect blend.

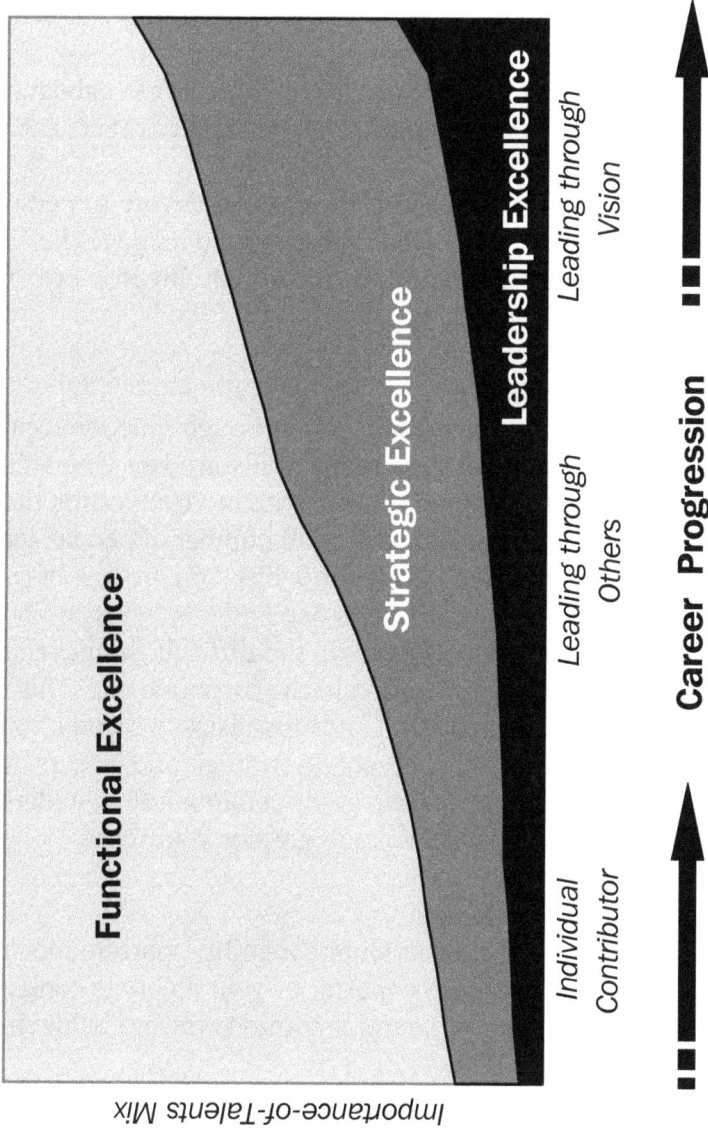

The Changing Mix of Talents Required Through a Career

Importance-of-Talents Mix

Functional Excellence

Strategic Excellence

Leadership Excellence

Individual Contributor

Leading through Others

Leading through Vision

Career Progression

Functional excellence

When you first get the job, it is normal to rely on your personal, direct contribution to manage performance.

Most people are good individual contributors. Those with strong functional skills outperform expectations and stand out from the crowd.

A small number of individual contributors, let's say about fifteen to twenty people out of a hundred, do better than others and move on to management roles.

As general manager, limit the time you devote to personally managing projects. Empower your people to manage the routine parts of execution and guide them through. Invest more of your own time to strategic issues.

Strategic excellence

For the successful general manager, although functional capabilities are still important, leadership skills are key. The ability to manage, to lead through others, becomes more important than the personal capacity to produce. A small number of people, let's say two or three, will make it to the top jobs. You are one of them!

Focus your time and effort to do the difficult things related to strategy. Link your organization to the corporate one. This is one of the "musts" to keep in mind and emphasize. A second "must" is even more difficult: taking corporate strategic and leadership concepts and translating them into easily communicated, understood, and implemented actionable strategies for your team.

Leadership excellence

In top executive jobs, functional capability matters much less. Leadership skills are more important—your ability to consistently move a large number of hearts and minds toward achieving the company goals.

The more time you are on a job, the more time you should be devoting to managing through leadership rather than personal involvement in execution. The more quickly you devote your time and effort to leading, the more confident and secure you are going to feel.

How can you play these three roles interchangeably, with ease and efficiency, day-in and day-out?

Depending on the business cycle and the issues you are facing at any specific point, adjust your time accordingly to spread your time between individual contributor and leader.

For example, sometimes you need to dive deep into managing, but at the same time you need to be agile and flexible enough to jump out of it into leadership as the situation demands.

I have never seen any successful general manager who was able to focus on only two out of the three excellence components. You need to be able to deal with all three aspects and do so interchangeably.

Routine-Management Systems

Does the day go by so quickly that you don't get many things done?

Do you lose time on less-important or routine things and spend late evenings or weekends doing quality work on strategic issues?

It is common that less important, routine activities consume the bulk of time and, unfortunately, energy, taking time and focus away from more-important, business-critical matters.

Common examples of such routine issues are:

- Requests by others to do something for them, all unplanned. These are the brief calls and the small requests by colleagues and friends. The inability to say *no* to them and lack of discipline are major causes for the time lost on such types of activities. It shows lack of discipline in managing time. Five or six such calls each day can easily take away a full hour, or twelve percent of the workday.

- Poor planning for following up projects and other activities also drains time. Poorly managed follow-ups, either as face-to-face meetings or teleconferences, often take much longer that initially planned. A three-minute planned call usually lasts ten to fifteen minutes. Multiply that by the eight or ten follow-ups that you might have to do on any given day and see how easy it is to waste a couple hours, or twenty to twenty-five percent of your workday.

• Urgent issues that come along or meetings on important matters often last much longer than initially planned.

The following systems help you manage routine effectively:

1. "To Do List": a simple and extremely important prioritization tool of daily activities.

2. "Managing your Calendar": basic guidelines and tips for optimum time allocation.

To Do List

The "To Do List" is what the name simply states: a listing of all the activities you know you have to do for the day.

First, list all items without omitting a single one.

Then prioritize them according to urgency and importance (rating them on a one-to-ten scale or categorizing them as A, B, and C activities).

Start working by following the prioritization list.

How often do you update the "To Do List"?

Update this list at midday, including any new activities that might have appeared within the morning. That way, you have an always up-to-date, rolling list.

How can you start?

Use a simple piece of paper or any type of electronic device with a note-taking feature (palm, electronic agendas, mobile phones).

Well-organized general managers update their electronic calendars three or four times per day, prioritizing and re-prioritizing their activities as the day moves along.

Managing the Calendar

Effective calendar-management enables optimum time-allocation through identifying the activities that take big chunks of your time (meetings, teleconferences, personal time, etc.) and allocating time according to the priority of each activity (see "To Do List").

Identify and prioritize the important meetings

When you include meetings in your calendar, prioritize them according to their importance, the participants, and the processes they will require.

- Importance of the issue. Deal first with the most burning issue, not the easiest or shortest ones. The more you postpone dealing with the tough issue, the more anxiety you will have and the less effective you will be when you finally deal with it. In addition, delaying dealing with the burning issue can put you at a disadvantage if the issue worsens while you are postponing dealing with it.

- Participants. Prioritize those meetings that include your boss and higher-ups.

  Deal first with the meetings that include people with whom it is difficult to reschedule. That could include main customers, industry-association heads, government representatives, etc.

  If you have a conflict between meeting your boss or meeting with a customer for an equally important issue, choose to meet with the customer. But be smart: let your boss know about your choice. He will understand, support, and appreciate it.

- Process. Respect the meeting-planning that others do. Don't ask for a change in the time or place just because of your own poor planning. Don't expect others to remind you to confirm your participation in a meeting.

  When you receive an invitation for a meeting, check your calendar and reply immediately.

  Do you have a real conflict and need to reschedule a meeting that someone else is setting up? Do it early and do it without noise, working with the assistant of the person who is organizing the meeting.

Block time for managing routine issues

Set aside thirty minutes to an hour each day in your calendar for all those brief but important phone or courtesy calls you need to make. They may not be urgent, but they are important for keeping relationships alive, which can be helpful in the long term.

Block time for yourself

Allow one or more hours every day for yourself.

Block your calendar so people will not have access to you. Use this time for doing the work you have to manage on your own.

When you travel, block out at least one or two hours in the schedule for emails and phone calls.

By doing that, you will always stay in touch with developments and manage the workload that otherwise would be waiting for you when you return to the office.

Giovanni's Case
Giovanni Tardelli, South Europe VP
Logistics/Distribution, Milan, Italy

Giovanni has improved his efficiency drastically by blocking time for himself during travel and recommends it without reservations.

"My job requires me to travel fifty percent of my time across my region. In the past, the meeting agenda was managed by the local country business heads who, wanting to benefit the maximum from my presence in their market, would fill my ten-hour days with their country-related meetings.

"That resulted in my spending an additional two to three hours each night just catching up on my emails and important calls. Even worse, the workload waiting for me back in the office in Milan would be so high that it would take me at least one day to catch up after every trip to my region.

"What I did about it:

"I asked my country heads to include in the agenda of each day of my visit in their countries two hours for me to do my office work.

"That increased my ability to catch up on things and increased my ability to manage time dramatically.

"Now, I am coming back to my office in Milan after a four-day trip, and it feels like I have never left the office."

Empower your assistant

Give the responsibility of managing the calendar to your assistant. A capable and efficient assistant can help you tremendously. She or he can take lots of pressure from you and allow you to focus on substance instead of the time-management details.

Takeaways

- Successful leaders spend well over ten hours in the office. They do it because they love what they do, because they want to do more of it, and mainly because they know it will further their careers. If you work long hours only because of insecurity and fear, you might want to get some advice from your mentor or your boss.

- Great general managers manage their time by moving so swiftly and naturally from mode to mode that no one knows when they are doing execution or strategy or leadership.

- Don't be fooled! Managing the calendar can be one of the most strategic things you do. You prioritize, focus, and allocate your time effectively. Is there anything more strategic than this? Think of the opposite...!

In Chapter Thirteen you learned how to manage your professional and personal time.

In the next chapter you'll look at organizational performance, specifically setting effective targets.

14

*Don't use current performance levels as the standards to meet.
Use them as the absolute minimum standards to beat.*

Ensure High Performance:
Set the Right Targets

How do successful general managers achieve targets?
They achieve them on time.

They achieve them in a timely fashion and do not stretch their organization by trying to catch up at the last minute.

They achieve them utilizing the initially planned resources. They do all of the above consistently, year after year.

Success is measured against objectives, or targets. The better you deliver your targets and the more consistently you do it, the more you will distinguish yourself from the pack.

Is delivery of targets so important?
Delivery is the most important measurement of success. Even if everything else fails around you, your boss dislikes you, and your people jump ship, your consistent delivery will still make the difference between your being a good general manager and a great one.

You cannot deliver, however, if the targets to be delivered are wrong.

In this chapter, you will learn the importance of target setting and learn systems for setting the right targets. You will see how to avoid the traps that can compromise the performance of your unit and your personal success.

Performance is benchmarked by delivery compared to the targets, by performance compared to the performance of similar business units within the company, and by performance compared to the competitive environment of your business unit.

It may sound strange, but outperforming your internal competitors—the other general managers in your company—might even be more important than beating your competitors in the market.

Successful general managers consistently overachieve on their targets across all these different benchmarking areas.

Do you want to be a great general manager?

Manage carefully the following methods for delivering and achieving high performance consistently:

1. Influencing the process of target setting
2. Finding the right balance of resource-allocation
3. Maximizing investment in advertising and promotion

Let's look into the first part: *Ensure high performance consistently by influencing the process of target setting*

Danny Thorniley, Senior Vice President for the Economist Corporate Network, describes it perfectly: "The secret to success in one's business and love life is the same: managing expectations… invariably downwards."

"We want to be Number One"

Name at least five companies that have a target to become Number Two or Number Three. It's difficult, isn't it?

Everybody wants to become Number one. And in most cases, Number One refers to sales, not company-market capitalization, profits, or ROI (Return on Investment) metrics, such as EVA (Economic Value Added or EBITDA (Earnings Before Interest, Tax, Depreciation and Amortization).

Why is everybody so passionate about being Number One? What is wrong with Number Two or three… or ten for that matter?

Goal setting is a managerial art. Good goal setters allocate and align resources in a sustainable manner over time in order to achieve their targets. That, in turn, leads to achieving company goals and fulfilling the company mission.

Wrong Goal/Target Setting

Why is setting over-aggressive targets risky?

Setting over-aggressive targets exposes the company to serious risks, such as overextending resources so severely that key people burn out while focus and alignment get lost.

It can also lead to losses of momentum when the final targets are missed.

Finally, it can result in the non-compliant activities of people or departments. Non-compliant in this sense means activities which are either unethical and/or not conforming to behavioral and policy framework that the company has set for all employees.

The wider the gap between targets and achievement, the higher the risk that people will revert to non-compliant activities in desperation to catch up.

The more aggressively the targets are set, the higher the expectation of employees, industry, and investors, and subsequently the higher the disappointment in case of failure.

A classic mistake managers make is to readjust their aggressive targets continuously when they realize they will not meet the initial targets. If you need to adjust targets, adjust them well and do it only once. If you cannot find the right target at midterm, it is better to stick with and miss a target. Don't change it multiple times without knowing where you are going.

Why setting low targets is not the right approach

Low, soft targets carry their own risks. They limit the company's potential and compromise the return on investment.

They also create a culture of low expectations and achievement based on sub-par performance.

Finally, they compromise the competitive positioning of the company, putting at risk its long-term survival.

How can you identify the right targets?

A rather simple but effective method to identify target limits is to continuously keep on raising the bar, the targets, on a quarterly basis until you just reach the targets or even have one or two successive periods of coming up short.

That way, you know how far you can stretch your organization, and you can adjust your target settings accordingly.

Be careful, however, as continuous adjustment of targets above expectations will result in successive target misses and eventually have a negative effect on your team's morale and momentum.

Right Goal/Target Setting

Setting the right targets is a key management objective. It should be done in a mature and wise spirit and be aligned with the capability of the company to achieve those targets.

Optimum targets should be aggressive and realistic.

Set ambitious, achievable targets higher than recent, actual results

Recent history is the best gauge of a company's ability to achieve targets. It neutralizes personal beliefs, expectations, and wishful thinking. Without limiting your ability to drive the company toward higher performance, always take a good look at the recent past and, unless a major plan, effort, initiative, or investment dictates otherwise, set goals not far away from the past actual performance.

Set targets with an awareness of the resources the company wants to invest towards achieving those goals

Resources need to be well-estimated and appropriately allocated toward the target activities. Assumptions about the availability of resources should be made following detailed and well-planned discussions with management, avoiding presumptions about investment levels that will not materialize and thereby put at risk the achievement of your target.

Continuously allocate resources toward the biggest business opportunities. Adjust targets across brands or services in a manner that is aligned with and focused on the changing patterns of targets.

Pay attention to the competitive environment in investment, promotion, innovation, and new product launches

Most targets are based mainly on internal assumptions about resources and growth without considering the competitors' moves. Companies usually assume that competitors will remain quiet in terms of investment- and resource-allocations, and thus they set targets without regard for what competitors may do. When the year starts and the competitors come in with an unexpected strategy, companies lose time, funds, and momentum just trying to adjust.

Examine possible competitive scenarios, prepare alternative action plans, and put them in action whenever a new competitive environment takes shape.

Estimate the changes and trends in the environment such as government policies, trade trends, and distribution channels

Markets change dramatically in short periods of time whenever major environmental or system changes shift consumer purchase behaviors and patterns.

The Internet revolution is the biggest and latest example. Thousands of opportunities were created for those who understood and acted on the possibilities and trends early enough. Amazon was one such success story.

Those who hesitated, like Barnes & Noble, lost opportunities and brought themselves into expensive and risky defensive positions.

For each opportunity created, an equal amount of loss is generated somewhere in the system. The opposite is also true.

Set targets according to the market potential, and use market share as the primary target-setting criterion

Relate targets to the business potential within a product category or geography. Use market share to guide you in setting your internal targets. A company without market-share targets is a company without a strategy.

Set targets that are ambitious but also realistically attainable

The management that sets the targets and the people who will work toward them should have the same expectations about achieving those targets. Targets that are ambitious but not attainable create disappointment. Usually, the first person to be disappointed is you, followed by your boss. But it's usually the sales force and marketing departments who pay for the disappointment with loss of bonuses and broken morale.

Tie targets to the right incentive plans

Don't do anything that you cannot measure, compare, or incentivize. Tie incentives to direct performance by employees in areas that the employees can personally affect.

Don't confine incentive plans to individual performance only, so that employees pay attention only to performance within their personal sphere and ignore the team good and spirit. Have a *team* incentive component as well to supplement the individual incentive plan.

Also, don't set only team and company objectives. It's important to encourage personal drive and focus and to boost the competitive spirit.

"If you strive for change, nothing will change if incentives and rewards do not reflect this." (Steve Allaire, Xerox)

Takeaways

- Set ambitious targets, but make sure they are realistic. Otherwise, someone will be disappointed; usually this someone is you, and usually it is the sales force who pays for the disappointment through losses of bonuses and declining morale.

- Missing miserably on over-aggressive targets is more damaging to the organization than over-delivering on less-optimistic targets, because morale is likely to be severely damaged.

- Adjusting targets lower or higher midway into the year is absolutely fine. Just make sure that you do it only once and that you do it well. If you adjust targets every month, targeting ends up meaning very little.

- Targets that are not measurable, comparable, and parts of an incentive plan are not targets. They are text material for bedtime reading.

Now that you appreciate the importance of setting the right targets, let's turn the attention to achieving these targets through efficient resource-allocation.

15

You can be in three types of businesses:
Spending money, saving money, and making money.
Which type is the right one for your business depends
on what you are managing: growth, decline, transition, or
status quo.
Get the combination right and win.

Ensure High Performance: Find the Right Resource-Allocation

How can you predict the sales from a new investment idea? When do you stop investing in a low-performing project? Is there such a thing as perfect balance in resource allocation?

In the previous chapter, you saw that setting the right targets is one of the three major parameters for achieving consistent high performance.

The next two parameters are:

• Finding the right balance of resource-allocation

• Maximizing advertising- and promotion-investment

In this chapter, we look into the second important parameter of beating your targets, "balancing resource-allocation for delivering top notch performance."

You will learn specific systems for optimum resource-allocation as well as techniques for monitoring and adjusting investment across brands, markets, and time periods.

Is there such a thing as a perfect balance of investment?
Technically, perfectly balanced investment does not and should not exist.

So many variables affect return on investment that perfect balance in investment is only a perception. An investment may seem to be balanced when you make it, because it is based on your business objectives, on the one hand, and on the competitive environment in which these investments are made, on the other. But things always change, including balance.

If perfectly balanced investments do not exist, then what should you be looking for?
The *right* balance. That's what.
The right balance is based on well-thought-out assumptions. Most importantly, it is a balance that everyone—management, you, your people—feels comfortable with and fully supports.
You cannot have the right balance of investment when your management or your people are not convinced and committed. They will jump ship as soon as the first difficulty comes along and leave you alone in the middle of the sea.

The job of the general manager is to find a balance that aligns divisional plans with those of the overall company, provides for the right focus of resources, and increases the commitment across the company...all while balancing short-term results and long-term expectations.

Allocate Resources Disproportionately and Maximize the Return on Your Investments

How do you maximize the allocation of your resources?
Do you invest in the same opportunities as you did last year?
Do you stop investing in low-performing projects? If so, how do you do that?

Deciding where to invest within your portfolio is key.

Resources for product support are not unlimited, so withstand the pressure to spread your resources equally across a wide portfolio range in the hope of providing a little bit of support to each product.

Right investment is disproportionate investment. Move the bulk of your resources to a smaller product portfolio.

Stop investing in low-performing, low-return ideas. Choosing which horses to run with is important, but choosing which horses to take out of the race is equally important.

Here is a system for optimizing resource-allocation through disproportionate prioritization

Identify your opportunities to grow and categorize them through a force-ranked approach.

Then, allocate your resources disproportionately from top to bottom according to the potential opportunity.

The table below gives an example of disproportionate resource-allocation through forced-ranking. Assuming a total of twenty possible investment opportunities, spread your resources to favor the higher-ranked ones.

Opportunity Rank	% of Investment Allocated
Top 5	40 – 50
Top 10	65 – 70
Top 15	90 – 95
Top 20	95 – 100

This approach can be applied to all resource allocation decisions, among products or services, across geographies, or among time periods.

Won't the sales from products that receive fewer resources dramatically decrease?

Contrary to what most managers believe, a decrease in investment does not usually correspond to a commensurate decrease of sales in affected products. For example, a decrease in investment by fifty percent on one product will not bring a fifty percent decrease in sales within the same year. Although this is not applicable to all industries and products, one can safely assume that the equity of a product does not just disappear precipitously. Product users, consumers, and clients do not change their usage habits immediately when your investment is cut.

To extend this further, a carefully planned schedule of decreasing investment will provide you with higher return on investment, because your sales will slide at a much slower rate.

The time period over which this can be exercised varies by the type of industry and the product equity. Promotion-sensitive sectors with low brand equity (e.g., Christmas gifts) are more likely to see quicker sales impacts than less promotion-sensitive industries with higher brand equity (e.g., expensive wrist watches).

Patrick's Case
Patrick Cook, Regional General Manager
Telecommunications, London, UK

Your marketing people will overemphasize the risks of the impact when you decrease investment in one brand. Resist it and take the risk.

"As my company was going through a major portfolio alignment, I was trying to convince our management in Belgium that the advertising budget behind some mature and well-established brands needed to be decreased in order to fund the future brands.

"Local management was furious over this approach with local 'experts' from the advertising agency supporting them. Their scenarios forecasted that the brand would decline immediately as soon as the advertising decrease of about twenty percent took place.

"Contrary to the local risk-averse proposals and utilizing data from similar activities in other markets, I asked the market to proceed with the advertising cut and confirmed to them that I would assume the full responsibility in case of failure of this strategy.

"My strategy paid off. A year after, not only had we achieved the savings envisaged, but the decrease in advertising budget minimally affected sales performance.

"This success, combined with the growth of the new brands that had received the additional advertising budget, led to a major increase in the overall growth and profitability of our affiliate in Belgium.

"How do you think the local management felt after the centrally dictated investment paid off against their strongly opinionated initial position? I can assure you they were more open to take risks the next time around..."

Cut Investments in Low-Performing Opportunities and Increase Your Focus on Priority Projects

The forced-ranking system above enables you to make cost-cutting decisions more easily and efficiently.

Simply start by cutting investment from bottom to top. Stop when you have accomplished the desired investment cuts and maintained an appropriate level of investment on the priority products, geographies, or seasons.

Six Steps to Achieve the Right Resource-Allocation and Maximize the Management of Your Investment Portfolio

Review the steps below. See how they apply to your company and how you can incorporate them into your budgeting and other investment-allocation and business-planning tools.

Learn from the previous business and investment plans

Compare current plans to last year's.

Evaluate in detail the successes or failures of the plans from the previous financial/investment period.

What results came from each investment? How successful was the resource-allocation? What are the lessons, both positive and negative, of the recent past?

Check the performance of specific activities compared to the initial targets. Dig deeply into what has worked and what hasn't. If an activity gave you ten last year, will essentially the same activity, conducted in essentially the same environment, give you twenty this year? What has changed?

Usually, you will find the only thing that has not changed is the wishful thinking of the planners, who have planned once again for the same conclusion of ten.

Add a page in each business plan to record the activities that will be different in this year's plan compared to the previous year. This list will show you how big a planned change is and whether this change justifies new performance expectations.

Avoid committing to projects of the past that had questionable results

If nothing major changes in the execution of an activity, why should you expect this same activity to give better results in the upcoming period? Double-check before you commit funds to projects that start with the description, "continue to . . .".

Look carefully at the year-to-date performance and the assumptions for each project in the future.

Set the right expectations

Set realistic performance expectations for new product launches and product innovations and improvements.

Avoid creating difficult-to-achieve or unrealistically low targets that can limit your potential achievement.

Companies are usually over-optimistic about the prospects for new products and innovations, about how fast they will be appreciated by the buyers, about the price consumers will be willing to pay for them, and about how long it will take competitors to catch up.

To avoid this, look at similar experiences in the past as well as what your competitors have done in similar circumstances while you place yourself in a position that takes realistic account of your own strength and environmental variables.

The first three months in the launch of a new product or product enhancement show with high degree of certainty the success this product or enhancement will have.

Several statistical models are available to provide accurate forecasts across the life cycle of your new product or enhancement. Pay special attention to the first period of any launch. It is not only the start of the life of your product, but it is the basis on which the future performance of the product can be projected.

Don't look for a perfect new opportunity each time; the best opportunity is the one you have in front of you now, still unexploited

Marketers will go out of their way trying to convince you of new promotional ideas or investments.

They will sound enticing, promising, at times revolutionary...

Should you share the excitement? Absolutely. But remain calm and temper your excitement by examining the numbers behind each assumption. If the numbers behind the analysis confirm the initial thoughts, then be excited.

Numbers don't lie; numbers will always point to the truth. The trick is to find the right numbers to use.

Respect performance milestones and be ready to stop investing when the deal turns sour

Every activity or project should have performance metrics aligned with the overall strategy of the company.

When results deviate significantly from expected targets and adjustments in execution do not bring positive change, be ready to cut your losses and to move your investment to other activities, as per your forced-ranked approach presented earlier.

Prepare a contingency plan and keep it active and updated

All businesses, industries, and companies operate in cycles with good and bad periods.

Good general managers understand this and prepare proactively by having contingency plans in place. These "what if" plans provide scenarios and hypotheses at various investment levels as well as plans to reallocate investments according to the changes dictated by industry trends or by headquarters.

By being proactive and ready to implement plans, you ensure better execution, avoid panic and overreaction, and ensure better resource-allocations under new sets of investment levels.

Take Aways

- The more disproportionately you allocate investment towards big opportunities, the higher your probability of maximizing performance.

- Stop feeding your slow horses and cut your investment in them to zero. Don't believe the risk-averse minds who will try to deter you by insisting that sales will also decline to zero. The stronger the equity of the brand, the longer the decline will take.

- "What is different compared to last year's plan?" The answer to this simple question will tell you how different the results will be compared to last year.

- Use numbers to compare resource-allocation results before you commit to new investments. Numbers don't lie. Even if it is someone's intention to gloss over reality, numbers will always lead to the truth. The trick is to find the right numbers to use.

You can now balance your resource allocations. In the next chapter you will learn how to optimizing your advertising and promotion budget to achieve top notch performance.

16

It is not the size of the competitor that matters; it is the size of the fight and how we go about it.

Ensure High Performance: Maximize Advertising and Promotion Investment

How much should you invest in advertising each brand? Should you do market research? And when? Before or after you invest?

"Our competitors are spending way more than us. We are at a serious disadvantage!" How many times have you heard this from your people?

In the previous two chapters you have analyzed two of the three major parameters in achieving consistent high performance: influencing the process of how targets are set and finding the right balance in resource allocation.

In this chapter we'll dive into the third and equally important parameter in ensuring high performance: maximizing advertising and promotion investment.

You will understand better the relation between advertising and promotion spending in building brand equity, you will see the importance of market research in maximizing investment, and you will learn systems for maximizing your investment output.

To maximize the return of your advertising and promotion budget, you need to coordinate the amount invested with how you invest it.

As direct product advertising and promotion is the single biggest variable expense across most industries, thoughtfully planned execution is key to the competitive vitality of your company, contributing to the survival and growth of both you and your company.

There are some basic strategies you can follow to reach the maximum efficiency of your advertising and promotion spending.

Invest in waves or cycles

Allocate your investment in waves over different time periods, varying your investment between heavier and lighter campaigns. Heavy investment periods form your major advertising wave, while lighter periods complement your heavy advertising by maintaining its impact.

How long should each wave be? How long should your total advertising and promotion investment be?

That depends on your advertising and promotion objectives, such as developing product awareness or intentions to buy. Secondarily, it also depends on the amount of competition you deal with in the marketplace.

Idle advertising periods, including periods with zero advertising activity, allow you to focus all of your spending into two or more heavier waves and give you better results than having a lighter campaign across the whole period.

Do market research for every activity you intend to invest in

Make market research a key element of your investment strategy. It helps you estimate the impact of a campaign and decide on an appropriate investment level.

Many companies treat their market research as a complementary activity, and most do not hesitate to cut their budgets when cuts are dictated. Such companies seriously compromise their ability to invest and monitor performance. Don't be one of them.

The tougher the environment, the higher your need to measure where and how you are investing.

How do you maximize the media-investment placements?

Advertising is a specialized skill. Expert planning is needed. So go to the experts. Go to your advertising or marketing agency. Most agencies are well equipped to provide you with quality services for a small part of your overall investment budget.

What are the major areas to research before investing in advertising?

Market research should fully cover user behaviors such as changes in usage and attitude, switches of users from and to your brand, as well as cultural peculiarities.

Woojung's Case
Woojung Kim, Business Unit Head Investment Banking, Seoul, Korea

"Part of my role is director for one line of investment products. I was asked to manage the launch campaign of this line in the Korean market.

"Our regional advertising agency was updating us on the pre-launch results of a market survey we conducted. All indicators were positive, but I still thought that one of the most critical elements related to 'intention to buy' was quite low when compared to other Asian countries with much-less-positive market characteristics, so I wanted to dig deeper into this.

"The agency shared with us a study that showed that what people 'intend' to do can vary greatly with what people 'actually' do, depending on the culture. If people around the various Asian countries show an intention to buy of, say one hundred percent, then the Filipinos will actually buy at eighty percent, Thais at ninety percent, and Koreans and Japanese close to a hundred percent. The Koreans do as they intend, whereas other cultures' behavior is more optimistic at the initial stages than when the actual decision takes place."

Benchmark your investment plans with those of your competitors

Advertising and promotion spending should be benchmarked against that of your major competitors and not be seen in isolation. Do not fall into the trap of planning your investment on the assumption that you have the only product out there. Do not assume that potential buyers will see only your advertising and that their intention to buy is judged in relation to your product only.

This false assumption can badly skew your expectations for the return on your investment.

How do you incorporate the competitors' plans into your analysis?

Make assumptions about the investment commitments of at least your two major competitors. Include assumptions about their plans, and measure the assumptions in terms of their effect on final buyer behaviors such as ability to buy and intention to buy.

With an ever-evolving and more complicated competitive framework, with ever-growing numbers of purchase options available to your ultimate buyers, and with ever-increasing similarities among products, it is a dreadful mistake to avoid including your competitors in your planning process.

For example, the intention of a customer to buy your product (e.g., a digital camera) can be compromised drastically by the offers of competing goods (e.g., a competitor with a reduced-price offer on similar product) as well as by the buyer's own discretion for spending his money on something totally different instead (e.g., a video recorder).

Measure everything before and after

Develop investment-performance metrics and monitor them at frequent intervals with the help of experts.

The ultimate measure of a promotional campaign may be the sales of the product, but sales alone cannot be the measurement of a specific advertising or promotional activity.

Metrics for each activity should be developed around technically driven criteria before the activity takes place (e.g., for media advertising measure GRPs [Gross Rating Points], frequency, and reach).

Equally, the actual results must be checked after the campaign has finished and compared against the initial campaign objectives.

Safeguard brand equity and invest accordingly

What is brand equity and why is it so tightly associated with your advertising and promotion efforts?

Equity is the value of your brand, both its perceived value in the minds of buyers and users as well as its actual value in dollars as estimated by the investment community.

The stronger the brand equity, the more established a brand is and the more difficult for newcomers to steal market share from the brand.

Formula

How can you measure the impact of advertising in your brand equity?

In addition to utilizing specialized media tools that your media or advertising agencies will develop for you, the following investment formula can be applied:

Assume that the A&P (advertising and promotion) performance is the result of the brand's equity, the brand's market share, and the amount spent in advertising and promotion.

Complete the formula for your brand and then do the same thing for your competitors' brands. See the how much A&P your competitor will need to invest to match your A&P performance.

Equity x Market Share x A&P Expenditure = A&P Performance

- Assign a weight to the equity of a brand up to 10, becoming larger according to the degree to which the brand is established.

- Multiply the equity factor by the brand's current market share.

- Multiply all by the level of A&P investment you plan to make.

Here is an example, comparing an established brand (A) and a newcomer brand (B):

	Brand A	**Brand B**
Equity	8	3
x Market Share	30	10
x A&P	200,000	1,600,000
= A&P Effort	48,000,000	48,000,000

(A&P: Advertising and Promotion)

As you can see, a new brand will need eight times the investment ($1.6 million) in order to match the A&P effort (factor of 48) that you have as a result of your high market share and your higher brand equity.

Use this formula to decide your own A&P investment. You might decide to lower investment in high-equity brands for a period or two and to reallocate this investment to your low equity brands in an effort to build them up.

You can also use this formula to persuade those people in your company who are sensitive to risk that some of your competitors will be spending more (e.g., as per the example above).

This formula brings reality into the investment process and offers a good answer to those who believe that new brands can be built overnight just by (over)spending.

This doesn't mean that miracles cannot happen with new brands. Sometimes they can jump to the top, even overnight. But remember these will be miracles; for everything else, you need to pay...and pay dearly!

Five Steps to Self Funding Your
Advertising and Promotion Investment

How do you react when your advertising or promotion budget is cut substantially? Is it a problem, or is it an opportunity?

If you believe you are the only one complaining to headquarters about your inadequate advertising and promotion budget, think again. Most managers make the same complaint and have the same concerns.

In a way, this is healthy! If a general manager states that he has enough investment, it means either that he is not searching enough for opportunities or that his company is throwing money away and could do the same job with less investment.

So what do you do when your company is forced to change plans and decides to cut your investment in the middle of your business year?

Effective general managers have contingency plans in place. You should have "what if" scenarios to cover abrupt and unplanned changes in strategies.

A system you can use to manage such cases is the "Business Building Funding."

Using this system, you identify such funds from your existing allocated investment and then you redistribute them across new business opportunities, depending on an even stricter prioritization on the biggest opportunities, based on the lower total investment.

For example, if twenty percent of additional investment comes from product or division A, all of those funds might go to product or Division B if the new business opportunity there is greater.

It is important to note that this mechanism takes place before the financial year starts and before your allocation to the various brands takes place.

This is how it works:

Step 1: Freeze a small percent (let's say five percent) of the overall advertising and promotional budget approved by your headquarters for the year. Do this as soon as the budget is approved and before the specifics of the budget planning are worked out.

By applying this freeze across all brands, you will insure that no specific unit feels too much of the impact and fair pressure is felt throughout your division. The time to announce and organize this is the beginning of each financial year so that investment planning can be done with the revised, lower advertising and promotion budget.

Step 2: As the year moves along, identify and put into the "Business Building Funds" any savings due to efficiencies created (e.g. the two or three percent savings you create from better purchasing of promotional items). This is in addition to the five percent frozen before.

Step 3: As each project is implemented, identify the savings that are due to poor execution (e.g., resources that have been cut from projects that were not completed on time without a good reason).

This would logically contribute an additional small percent (let's say another two or three percent.)

This two or three percent would be in addition to the eight percent identified from the frozen allocations and the efficiency discussed in steps 1 and 2 above. Total savings under this scenario would be ten percent or more compared to the initial budget approved by your management.

Step 4: Ask your business-unit heads or marketing team to identify additional business-building opportunities that could be captured using this additional investment of ten percent.

These additional business opportunities should come from new ideas or from applying heavier investment to existing, planned, or prospective good ideas.

Systems such as Business Building Funding can greatly increase the efficiency of advertising and promotional investments. But ownership by key stakeholders such as business-unit heads and marketing directors and step-by-step investment-monitoring is critical in making it work properly.

As Giovanni Caforio (Senior Vice President, EMEA, for Bristol-Myers Squibb Company) has said about A&P: "People need to feel responsible for managing the authority to spend on specific activities rather than assuming that they have the right to write a check for a million dollars or two after the budget approval has taken place."

Jim Atkinson (Director, Beckman Coulter International SA) agrees. For him "budget should never be an entitlement to spend."

Take Aways

- The advertising and promotion mission is to build brand equity. The higher the brand equity, the higher your long-term sales potential. This is where the focus should be. Sales is a critical parameter for building brand equity, but it should not be the mission itself.

- Market research is too often on top of the list of expenses to be cut by companies under budget constraints. Don't follow them. The tougher the environment, the greater the need to measure where and how you are investing.

- Decreases in advertising and promotion budgets should not be seen only as a limitation to competition. They are also opportunities. Encourage your people to come up with innovative plans and ideas to cover the spending gap, better investment opportunities, and more competitive investment-placement.

- If you believe that your current advertising and promotion budget is the maximum you should invest, think again. Either you are overspending or you have not captured enough opportunities in the market.

Technically challenging, it is nevertheless substance-critical to optimize advertising and promotional effort, because that is the key to the last chapter, which tells you how to beat your targets each and every time!

17

If something cannot be measured, compared, and incentivized, don't do it.

Seven Systems To Beat Your Targets Each And Every Time

Are targets in your company driven from the top down, with management allocating to the various business units what they wish to achieve at total company level?

Do you and your management share the same understanding about the difficulty of achieving your targets, or does management believe it will be easier for you to hit your targets than you do?

Budgeting is the single most important business-planning process, because it states the business assumptions for a given period of time. A good budget includes at minimum:

- The objectives to be achieved and the resources to be allocated by the company for achieving those targets

- A detailed list of the assumptions upon which these objectives were based

- The investment rationale in terms of the human and promotional items required to attain the set targets

- Performance metrics for the milestones to be achieved, the timing within which each milestone is to be reached, and the results of meeting the milestones

- Contingency plans in case market, company, or product trends necessitate the change of investment strategy

Budgeting is also the main performance-monitoring tool, so it forms the basis on which bonuses and incentives are awarded and the metric for your personal career performance and advancement.

How do most companies budget?

Most companies follow a conservative process of budgeting based on negotiation between each operating unit or division and central management or headquarters.

What is wrong with this approach and why should it be avoided?

It is negotiated. Top management usually asks for more than the various business units can offer. Business units provide less than what they can actually achieve because they understand the bargaining process in front of them and they want to start the process from the low end.

At the end of the day, one side starts at 110, the other at 90. Eventually they meet around 100 and they are both happy.

It is mainly internal. Targets are based mainly on top management needs and do not necessarily reflect the ability of the various business units to achieve those targets in a timely manner.

If headquarters expects that your targets will increase by at least ten percent across the world as a result of a new product introduction and you are in Taiwan where the local government has just imposed price constraints or a ban on new product introductions, you have a problem. The gap is going to be sizable.

Everybody gets a fair share of the boss's target pie. When your boss gets a target, he/she allocates it across the business units or regions he is managing.

You get your share based on your past performance (you might get "punished" with tougher targets if your previous performance was better than others . . .) or according to the expected potential of your business unit (even if it is projected by headquarters without regard for local variables that can affect your ability to achieve or exceed the targets).

In most companies, the budgeting process does not roll over time. The budget is tied to the financial year, the twelve-month reporting period that the company works under.

However, markets—consumers, users, behaviors—neither understand nor abide by that, so why should budgeting give us the impression that each new financial year is a separate entity with a beginning point and an end?

Budgeting should roll, applying an evolutionary process every quarter and revising assumptions and corresponding plans without disrupting the business. Every quarter you should renew and extend your budget coverage for another quarter. For example, if your company's budgeting process covers a yearly period of twelve months, then as each quarter passes, you should plan for a period of a full twelve months by including one more quarter in your planning process.

Seven Systems That Beat Your Targets Each and Every Time

Understand the corporate budget model...then beat it

Check the corporate timelines for budgeting. Plan your own time-table around the corporate one, but do it more aggressively.

- *Set early budget-preparation deadlines.* Start each phase of the budget-planning process earlier for your unit so you have more time for reviews, adjustments, and contingency planning. Bringing target deadlines earlier by even one week provides you with plenty of room to do more thorough analyses and to prepare pre-emptive contingency plans.

- *Set more-aggressive targets.* Increase each target by a small increment, depending on the possibility you have to improve performance. That applies to every target area, including investments and expenses, not just sales.

- *Do pre-budgeting exercises.* Using main strategy and financial indicators, do a summary analysis of no more than three pages. Well-prepared snapshots give you a good idea of overall trends and assumptions and help you identify potential opportunities and make resource-allocation decisions.

  A pre-budgeting exercise will also help you create several "what if" scenarios or hypotheses and give you a more complete plan for improving your performance. It will also improve your preparation for the final discussions with management.

  The pre-budgeting strategy elements can include success factors related to environment and brands, main strategic thrusts, or the main strategies you plan to utilize for attaining your objectives.

  The pre-budgeting financial indicators can include year–by-year sales, gross margin, and brand-contribution trends for key brands, total-market-share trends, and price and volume projections (actual and assumptions).

Manage the assumptions included in the budgeting process

All budgeting, forecasting, and planning involves assumptions. Actually, this is what budgeting is about: the assumptions address the expectations and the means to achieve those expectations.

How well you know the assumptions, how broad your assumptions are, and how you communicate them to management will be critical for getting fair and achievable budget targets.

- The golden rule in managing assumptions is that the less you know about an area you plan to invest in, the less control you have over this area, and the broader the assumptions you must make. The opposite is also true and should be considered in your strategy: the more you know about the assumptions, the

BUDGETING – ASSUMPTIONS MAPPING

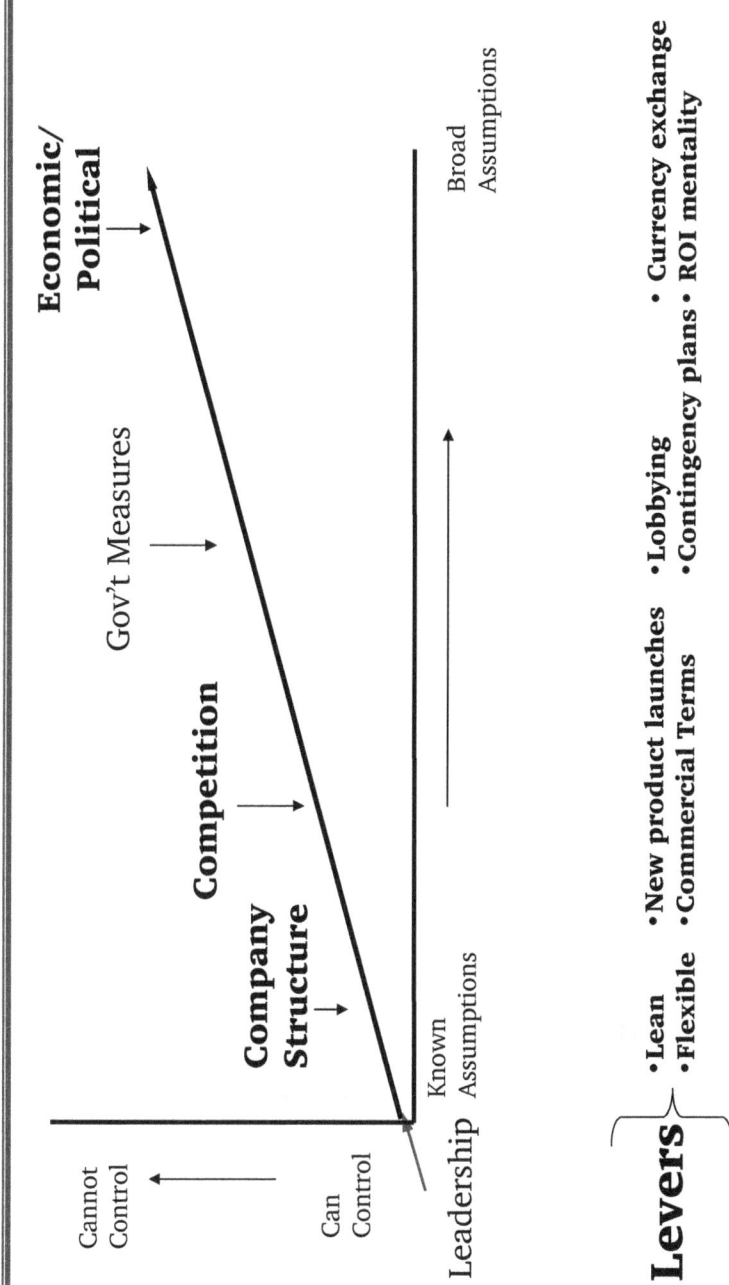

Cannot Control

Can Control

Leadership   Known Assumptions

Company Structure

Competition

Gov't Measures

Economic/ Political

Broad Assumptions

Levers
- •Lean
- •Flexible
- •New product launches
- •Commercial Terms
- •Lobbying
- •Contingency plans
- •Currency exchange
- •ROI mentality

more control you have over them and the tougher and tighter your strategy should be.

List the major areas, factors on which assumptions need to be based. These can include structure (organizational related matters, resources, etc.), competition, government activities, and economic parameters (e.g., cost of money).

- The Y-axis marks the degree of control or influence you have over each factor, moving from your organization, where theoretically you have the maximum control, to the environment (e.g., government), where you have the least control.

- The X-axis maps out the precision of the assumptions you should take for each area. At the base of the axis, your planning assumptions are very strict, aggressive, and well-defined in terms of internal resources and organizational capabilities, since these are things you have power to manage on your own. As you move along the X-axis, however, you need to make wider, more conservative assumptions, simply because your knowledge and ability to influence are more limited.

- In assumption mapping, you then proceed to adjust your levers (the main strategic drivers) to link this map to your strategy and execution plans.

Manage management expectations by creating them

How much input do you give management when it sets your unit's targets?

Anticipating and beating management expectations about targets can be easy, especially if management follows the conservative approach of yearly budgeting from the top down.

You create those expectations in the minds of your management throughout the year by means of a systematic approach.

- Start early in the year by reminding management about the volatility that exists in the environment where your business unit operates. You can refer to the most recent issues, problems, and crises that you faced, especially when those relate to the environment. Remember to emphasize the risks that stem from factors you cannot control, like government regulation and major competitive moves. For example, the volatility of the environment is higher in a market like Turkey than in a market like Canada. Your management knows that but also expects you to raise it as a concern.

- Communicate to key people in management the news articles or stories that refer to changes in competitive activities or industry issues. Change always coincides with risk, and by sending those messages on a frequent basis you start increasing the level of concern and risk. The closer you get to the formal budgeting process, the more frequently you should communicate that kind of news.

- Choose the area that is of particular concern to your business unit and remind management about its impact. It could be business units that have new operating committees in place or several new members. Or it could be an important company product or service where your competitors are heavily undercutting your price.

- Include headquarters in the task forces you form to manage your major challenges. These representatives from headquarters will communicate to their colleagues the volatility and risk surrounding your business, and hopefully they will observe and report your good management of the situation.

Incorporate contingency plans as key elements of your budget

Contingency is an integral part of any type of planning. In fact, the more volatility in a plan, the more important a sound contingency plan is.

Contingency refers to the strategies and plans a company has in place for times when things don't go the way initial assumptions and expectations predicted. Contingency refers to the "what if" scenarios and plans you put in place to manage variances and risks.

How do you create solid contingency plans?

- Anticipate the areas of risks and exposure, and have plans ready in case they are needed ("reactive plans"). Once you identify these areas of risks, quantify and monitor their development on a frequent basis.

- Perform a detailed evaluation of the risks and prepare your reactive plans. These plans need to go into great detail about resources and be ready to come off the shelf in case they need to be deployed quickly.

- Make sure you have the milestone deadlines on which you will make decisions about activating your contingency plans. The decision to activate can be taken at the end of each quarter or mid-year.

- Don't go wild with contingency plans. Make them simple to implement. Remember, if you decide to activate a contingency plan, this plan must be ready to be executed. You will not have time to prepare your organization fully, so you need simple and focused plans.

   A simple example could be a case of having a best- and a worst-case scenario to accompany your main plan.

   The most effective contingency plans are rolling in their nature. The general manager identifies the point when change or adjustment takes place once the contingency plan goes into effect. Then, depending on the situation, he adjusts the bar continuously as the issue or the success of the contingency plan dictates. For example, the less the impact in improving declining sales, the deeper you need to go into your contingency plan for allocating resources to other investment areas (if that was your initial plan).

- Manage the implementation of the plan tightly when you decide to proceed with it. As with any other project, strong sponsorship from upper management and good talent among the participants will increase the probability and extent of success.

Remember, a contingency plan must work. If it doesn't, the alternatives are usually less under your control; your performance will be damaged as you will be investing without a plan. At any rate, headquarters will tell you how to manage it, and that will mean you have even less control.

• Learn from it. Contingency plans go into place because the initial assumptions or plans did not work. Take the lessons, record them, and discuss them throughout the company so that you expand the knowledge base and improve future planning.

Be prepared to sacrifice one part of your targets in order to keep the momentum

Assume that despite all your efforts, your business unit has a target that seems unreachable and possibly unrealistic.

Challenge management to the point where your voice has been heard and heeded by the right people in the hierarchy. If targets don't change, accept it with your chin up. Then put plans in place to achieve it.

When you allocate your own divisional or company target across each one of your brands or sub-units, put the extra, non-realistic part of the target in only one brand or product category.

Sacrificing the success of one product in favor of more important targets may harm the chances of success for the sacrificed product. But it is preferable to spreading the risk across all of your products equally and limiting the probability for success for all products.

Placing a small part of your business at higher risk can be more easily managed than spreading the risk across your entire portfolio. Otherwise, the momentum of your organization will slow down and affect negatively the morale of your people.

You could make adjustments to improve the prospects of the sacrificed product by adding additional resources, but do this only when you see other products performing over-budget and/or the market trends for the product under pressure are changing favorably.

Walter's Case
Walter Billington, Business Unit Head
Fast-Moving Consumer Goods, U.K.

Walter had received a seemingly unrealistic total-division target for the year. He managed to keep momentum and performance high in his organization, but he did so by sacrificing the target achievement on one specific product line.

"I thought I had done a good job in presenting my budget assumptions for the following year, but finally I received an overall sales target for my division that seemed impossible to achieve.

"I knew that spreading the pressure across all brands would simply create a major stretch for all people, leading to under-achievement and loss of momentum, and I did not want this to happen.

"I chose to put the part of the total target that seemed un-reachable on one of the brands which was large in size but in a very volatile competitive environment which made the chances of achieving targets on this product remote, anyway.

"With realistic targets on the other brands, we had a very good first half, overachieving targets and having promising trends.

"Looking at this positive trend mid-year, I increased the targets in the well-performing brands, which gave me the opportunity to formally lower the targets of the overstretched one. People behind this brand started feeling good as their targets were now more realistic and their performance started to improve.

"We did not quite manage to achieve our initial target that headquarters set for the product under stretch. But having achieved our overall division target, all people were content, felt and were successful, including the people working on the product with the stretched targets."

Set a ten percent margin of fat on top of your internal targets. Then, forget about them

You have received your targets and they are stretched and tough to achieve. Your efforts to manage assumptions and create realistic expectations has worked.

It is now up to you to allocate those targets among products and spread them across the year in a way that balances the stresses across all of them.

Here are some guidelines:

- *Increase the target before you announce it to your teams.* People adjust their efforts according to the objectives they have been assigned. They will easily incorporate a slight increase of the budgets upwards, and their mindsets will be adjusted to reflect the new target.

  For example, add a small percent of, say, five to ten percent spread equally across brands.

  That way, you create a leverage, a filter between internal target-setting and your commitment to headquarters. This will give you an additional push and increase your probability of success.

- Allocate targets on a quarterly basis based on actual results in the past as well as trends developing today. *But push achievement towards the earlier part of the year.*

  For example, assume that you expect your sales to be twenty-five percent per quarter over four quarters for the year. Try to accelerate it by bringing performance earlier in the year, as follows:

  1Q: 28%   2Q: 27%   3Q: 25%   4Q: 20%

  That way, you achieve a good ratio on your overall targets by mid-year (five percent over the budget performance) and then, with much less pressure on numerical performance, you can focus attention on more qualitative work, such as development and training programs for your people or pilot testing ideas, concepts, new products, etc.

Depending on your industry, the percentages of allocation will depend on the seasonal nature of each business as well as other critical parameters, such as governmental spending cycles.

• Balance out targets and pressure across products.

Revise your targets and their allocation on a quarterly basis by balancing out the pressure across products or sub-units. Increase the future quarterly targets on products with better-than-expected performance and lower the targets on products that have a tougher time and cannot meet their targets.

Set incentives to achieve targets and keep momentum high

Incentive systems are performance-management tools and key components of successful teams.

Good incentive systems are used to set the right tone, to create and sustain momentum, and most importantly, to balance pressure across brands, geographies, and teams.

A sound incentive plan covers the following areas:

Duration: Depending on the business you are in and the way your company is organized, incentives can be yearly, quarterly, or monthly.

The shorter the duration, the tighter the connection between performance and incentives.

You can also choose to have a combination of incentives that include both short- and long-term objectives, with the emphasis always being on the shorter-term ones.

Flexibility: Incentives should be adjustable within the year as the targets evolve. If a target is not reachable due to factors other than the performance of people or teams, you should adjust incentives to provide fair rewards to the participants.

Flexibility allows the company or business units to balance the pressure across brands, teams, or time periods within the performance year. For example, if Team A is below its targets by twenty percent in the first quarter but Team B is up by fifteen percent, then the targets of Team A can be adjusted downwards to become more realistic while those of Team B can be adjusted upwards to reflect its previous performance.

This provides a fair and balanced adjustment of pressure moving forward into the year.

A Cap: Incentives should be based on a maximum ceiling of performance and benefits. Whether this cap will be at 130 percent or 160 percent depends on the business you are in, the size of the business you are managing, and the volatility expected. For mature markets, for example, I believe that 130% is generally a fair ceiling for most businesses.

A ceiling is necessary, since an employee can perform up to 30 percent better due to his own contribution; people can work 20–30 percent harder, smarter, or more systematically, but it is rather difficult to believe that people perform at 200 percent. That can mean only that targets were set too low or market trends changed very favorably. In either case, the high performance was due to circumstances, not design or effort.

A cap on performance is also an important control mechanism. A cap keeps unethical behavior under control, as some employees may use means that are not acceptable or desirable to get higher-than-expected performance for selfish reasons.

A balance between individual versus team contribution: All plans should have individual and team components; each employee needs to be incentivized for the areas he/she is directly responsible for, yet the team should account for twenty-five to fifty percent of the overall incentive.

As closely as possible, incentives should be based on the areas an employee can personally affect; otherwise, the individual contribution is lost in the overall team or company performance and interest in performing better is lost.

Measurement of what is important: For the commercial departments in the organization, numerical targets should include sales, market share, and profitability, at the minimum.

The right balance among these three elements depends on the business and the focus the company has set for itself.

Behaviors: Behaviors for achieving ethical performance and practice should also be targeted appropriately, measured, and included in the overall incentive plan.

Behavioral elements include: alignment to the strategy, team spirit, pursuit of the overall strategy, compliance, ability to innovate, etc.

Performance kickers: Kickers are used when focus and attention need to be directed to a specific brand during one period of time more than during others. Performance kickers can be used during a new product launch or during a major promotional campaign, for example.

Kickers are limited in both duration and the size of the reward.

They should be an integral, ongoing element of the overall incentive plan.

Benchmarking target achievement across sales reps: You know you have set targets correctly when seventy-five to eighty percent of your total sales representatives are performing at close to a hundred percent of their targets, while only ten to fifteen percent are coming up short. That means that ten to fifteen percent of your people are missing their target and, yes, this is healthy and strategic.

If, for example, more that forty percent of your people are overachieving targets, you have set very low targets.

If, on the other hand, forty percent of your people are missing targets, you have set overly aggressive targets and risk losing momentum and profits!

Take Aways

- Don't try to be a hero during the period when budgets are being negotiated with your management. Don't promise the stars or you will end up disappointing them. In turn, they will disappoint you when your performance-review time comes. Offer headquarters ambitious but realistically attainable targets, and be a hero by exceeding them.

- Beat your internal company competitors: the other general managers or business-unit heads. In most companies this is more important for career-development than beating your competitors in the marketplace where you compete. Of course, you cannot beat your internal competitors without doing well in the marketplace.

- Don't put incentives on everything your people sell. This dilutes the incentive focus away from your big-ticket items. Allocate incentives disproportionately toward the biggest opportunities. If you achieve targets on the big items, you will more than cover any losses you might have on the smaller ones.

- See contingency planning as a key element of your budgeting process, not as an "in-case-things-go-wrong" plan. Use contingency plans when things go differently from the initial plans, which is the case most of the time.

Final Word

Now that you know proven and innovative systems for maximizing performance, it is time to put them to work for you.

Implementing what you read in this book will be more challenging than reading about it, but it will also be more enjoyable and rewarding.

Go for it.

Acknowledgements

I thank the great general managers from around the globe who have contributed their personal experiences openly and unselfishly:

Jim Atkinson, Dennis Chia, Ronald Bruhin, Roberto Giusti, Nicolas Portier, Elena Trenton, Suzuki Aoki, Hedan Jerome, Christopher Foster, Eduardo Morales, Van Der Wooden Willem, Ahmed Abdalla, Danniel Barnes, Sean Allen, Vladimir Petrovic, Danny Wilson, Giovanni Tardelli, Daeun Lee, Kanzaki Tohko. Jonathan, Lohre, Woojung Kim, Jordi Vasquez, Harry Patel, Antonio Morales, John Curtis.

Special Thanks to Edel Aubier, George Panagakis, Pascal Roux, and Dimitri Karavasilis for keeping me going at it and their friendship.

High appreciation goes to book coach Judy Cullins <*www. bookcoaching.com*> and book designer Bob Goodman <*www. silvercat. com*> for guiding me through this book.